ELEMENTARY ALGEBRA

Grades 1 - 2

by Marcia Dana

Carson-Dellosa Publishing Company, Inc.
Greensboro, North Carolina

Credits

Editor: Amy Gamble
Layout Design: Tiara Reynolds
Inside Illustrations: J.J. Rudisill
Cover Design: Annette Hollister-Papp
Cover Illustrations: Annette Hollister-Papp

ISBN 1-59441-192-1

Table of Contents

Introduction

This book focuses on many of the early algebra concepts described in the NCTM Algebra strand. The activities in this book are designed to expand students' mathematical understanding, particularly in the area of algebra. A variety of developmentally appropriate activities will help students become familiar with the following elementary algebra skills:

- number and shape patterns
- skip counting
- functions
- equality and inequality
- comparing sets
- writing number sentences
- solving number sentences
- properties of numbers
- investigating change with graphs and tables
- variables

Each concept is presented in an easy-to-understand way that is intended to be both interesting and fun for students. This book can be a valuable tool in helping students achieve growth in their mathematical development.

Name _____   Date _____

Sorting

Directions:

Cut out the boxes below. Paste the triangles inside the "triangles" set. Paste the squares inside the "squares" set. Paste any shapes that don't belong outside the sets.

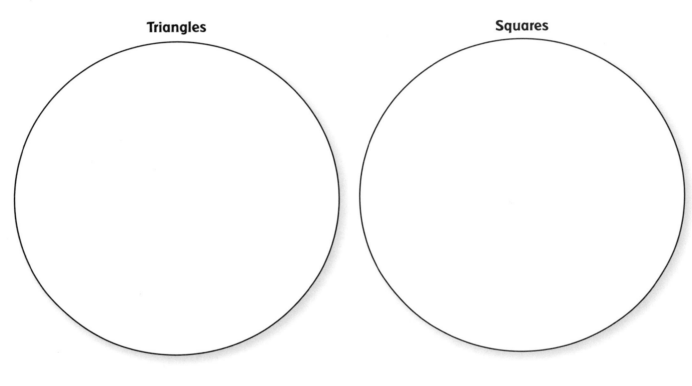

Triangles   **Squares**

How many boxes did you paste outside the sets? _____

Why didn't they belong inside either set? _____

_____

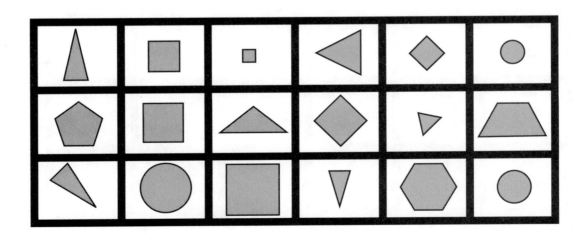

Sorting Letters

Sorting

Directions:

Cut out the boxes below. Paste lowercase letters inside the "lowercase" set. Paste uppercase letters inside the "uppercase" set. Paste any boxes that don't belong outside the sets.

Lowercase   **Uppercase**

How many boxes did you paste outside the sets? _____

Why didn't they belong inside either set? _____

_____

D	g	C	4	B	E
F	G	a	e	<u>d</u>	<u>6</u>
3	<u>b</u>	A	c	f	5

Sorting Numbers

Directions:
Cut out the boxes below. Paste the numbers inside the correct sets. Paste any boxes that don't belong outside the sets.

Numbers Less Than 10

Numbers Greater Than 10

How many boxes did you paste outside the sets? _____

Why didn't they belong inside either set? _____

_____

6	20	52	1	30	10
100	4	13	25	8	5
15	2	7	0	3	12

More Number Sorting

Directions:

Write the numbers on the left in the correct sets.

A.

6	5	8	2
3	4	7	10
15	24	37	41
1	11	25	36

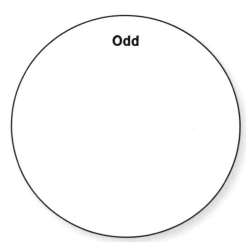

Even

Odd

B.

11	6	12	2
100	50	1	8
0	10	5	3
4	9	15	20

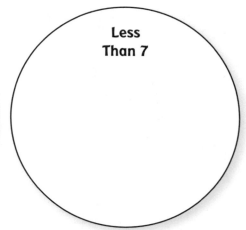

Greater Than 7

Less Than 7

C.

21	52	42	22
5	12	38	3
2	24	62	32
19	200	72	162

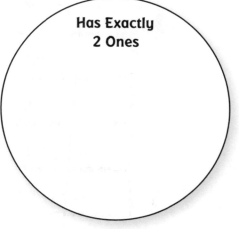

Does Not Have Exactly 2 Ones

Has Exactly 2 Ones

Secret Sorting

Classifying

Directions:

Some things have been sorted into sets. Cut out and paste each set name under the correct set.

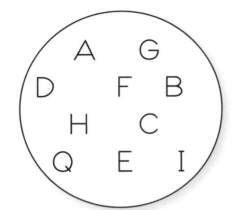

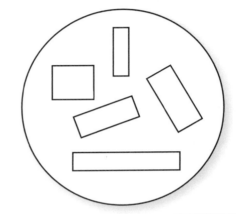

1. _____

2. _____

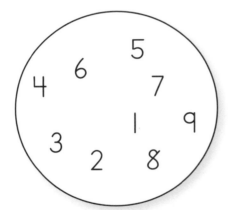

3. _____

4. _____

all frowns	all rectangles
all smiles	all triangles
all uppercase letters	numbers greater than 10
all lowercase letters	numbers less than 10

Elementary Algebra • CD-104104

More Secret Sorting

Classifying

Directions:
Some numbers have been sorted into sets. Cut out and paste each set name under the correct set.

6   8
20   12
10   22   2
18   24
16
4   14

95   74
63   90
82   51
67
58   75
86
97   55

1. [ ]

2. [ ]

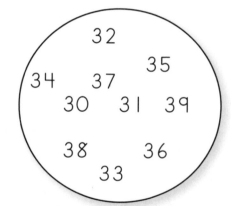

32
35
34   37
30   31   39
38   36
33

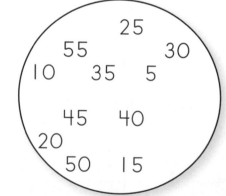

25
55   30
10   35   5
45   40
20
50   15

3. [ ]

4. [ ]

odd numbers	5 in the ones place
even numbers	numbers greater than 50
3 in the tens place	answers when counting by 5
5 in the tens place	answers when counting by 10

Name _____ Date _____

Weird Cookies

Directions:
Jan made cookies with her new cookie cutters. Count how many sides each cookie has. Then, answer the questions below.

_____ sides	_____ sides	_____ sides	_____ sides	_____ sides

H	**S**	**T**	**O**	**P**
hexagon cookie	square cookie	triangle cookie	octagon cookie	pentagon cookie

1. Which cookie has the fewest sides? _____

2. Which cookie has the most sides? _____

3. Write the cookie letters in order of the number of sides the shapes have.

_____ _____ _____ _____ _____

fewest sides   **most sides**

4. How many more sides does O have than H? _____

5. How many more sides does H have than S? _____

6. How many fewer sides does T have than P? _____

7. How many fewer sides does S have than O? _____

8. How many more sides would P need to become O? _____

Clowning Around

Ordering

Directions:

Each clown's shoe is a different length. Write the clowns' names in order of the lengths of their shoes. Write the first set in order from shortest to longest. Write the second set in order from longest to shortest.

You

Sou

Bou

Zou

_____   _____   _____   _____

shortest shoe   **longest shoe**

• •

Ned

Ted

Hed

Zed

Red

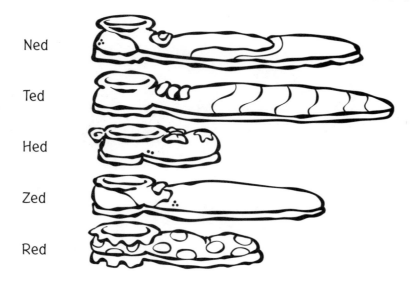

_____   _____   _____   _____

longest shoe   **shortest shoe**

Name _____ Date _____

More Clowning Around

Directions:
Each clown's hat has a letter name. Look at the heights of the hats and answer the questions using the letter names for the hats.

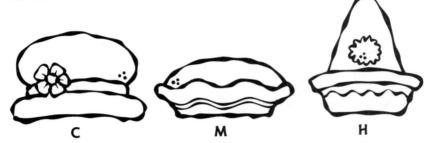

C   M   H

1. Which hat is the tallest? _____

2. Which hat is the shortest? _____

3. Write the hats' letter names in order from shortest to tallest.

_____   _____   _____

4. Circle the number sentences that are true about the hats. Remember: > means greater (taller) than, < means less (shorter) than, and = means equal to.

C > M	H < C	M > H	C = H
H > M	M < H	C < M	H > C

   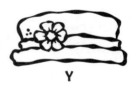

Z   A   N   Y

5. Write the hats' letter names from tallest to shortest.

_____   _____   _____   _____

6. Circle the number sentences that are true about the hats.

Z > Y	Z > A	A > Y	A < Y	A = N
N < A	Y > Z	N > Z	A < Z	Z < N

Name _____

Date _____

Striped Snakes

Directions:

Each snake has a color pattern. Color the lettered sections. Then, continue the pattern.

R is red.　　　G is green.　　　B is blue.　　　Y is yellow.

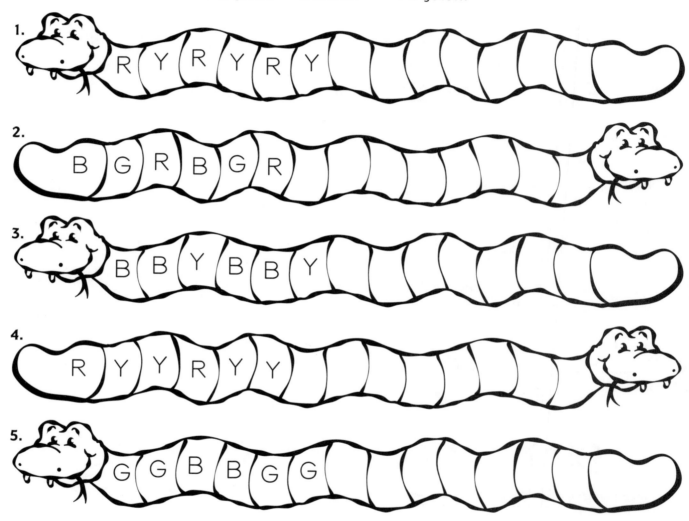

1. R Y R Y R Y

2. B G R B G R

3. B B Y B B Y

4. R Y Y R Y Y

5. G G B B G G

Make your own pattern.

6.

ABC Patterns

Extending Patterns

Directions:
Write the correct letters to continue each pattern.

1. | A | B | A | B | A | B | | | | | | | | |

2. | C | D | D | C | D | D | C | | | | | | | |

3. | E | E | F | E | E | F | E | E | | | | | | |

4. | G | H | H | H | G | H | H | H | | | | | | |

5. | I | I | J | J | I | I | J | J | | | | | | |

6. | K | L | M | K | L | M | | | | | | | | |

7. | N | N | O | P | N | N | O | P | | | | | | |

8. | Q | R | S | T | Q | R | S | T | Q | | | | | |

Black and White Patterns

Extending Patterns

Directions:

Shade or draw lines to continue each pattern.

1.

2.

3.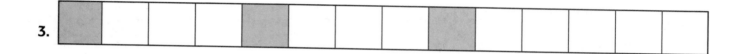

4.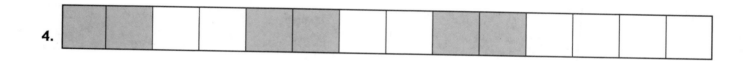

5.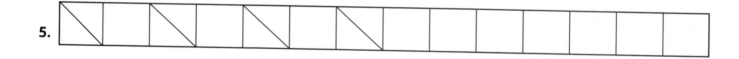

6.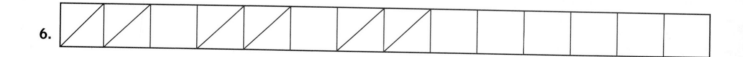

7.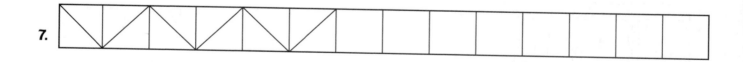

8.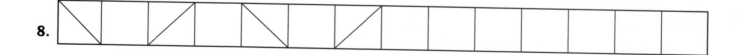

Alphablocks

Directions:
Lex made patterns with his alphabet blocks. For each pattern, tell what letter would come next and why.

1. A B C A B C A B C A B

What letter comes next? _____

Why? _____

_____

2. D D E D D E D D E D D

What letter comes next? _____

Why? _____

_____

3. F F G G F F G G F F G

What letter comes next? _____

Why? _____

_____

4. H I I H I I H I I H I I

What letter comes next? _____

Why? _____

_____

How Does It Work?

Describing Patterns

Directions:

Write a sentence about how each pattern works.

1.

_____

_____

2.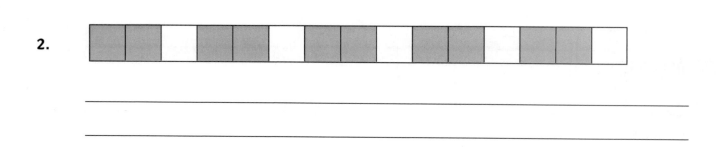

_____

_____

3.   A   B   B   B   A   B   B   B   A   B   B   B

_____

_____

4.   2   4   6   8   10   12   14   16   18   20

_____

_____

Make Your Own Patterns

Creating Patterns

Directions:

Choose two different colored crayons. Make two different patterns with the colors.

Directions:

Choose two letters of the alphabet. Make two different patterns with the letters.

Directions:

Choose two numbers. Make two different patterns with the numbers.

Change Up

Transforming Patterns

Directions:
Use letters, numbers, colors, shapes, etc., to make a new pattern that follows the same rule as each given pattern below.

1. | L | M | N | O | L | M | N | O | L | M | N | O | L | M |

| | | | | | | | | | | | | | |

2. | I | 3 | 5 | 5 | I | 3 | 5 | 5 | I | 3 | 5 | 5 | I | 3 |

| | | | | | | | | | | | | | |

3. | O | O | – | – | – | O | O | – | – | – | O | O | – | – |

| | | | | | | | | | | | | | |

4. | a | a | b | b | c | c | d | d | e | e | f | f | g | g |

| | | | | | | | | | | | | | |

Name _____   Date _____

Even Numbers

Directions:

Starting at 0, count by 2s to count the **even** numbers. Lightly shade each number you count.

0	1	2	3	4	5	6	7	8	9
10	11	12	13	14	15	16	17	18	19
20	21	22	23	24	25	26	27	28	29
30	31	32	33	34	35	36	37	38	39
40	41	42	43	44	45	46	47	48	49

1. What numbers do the even numbers have in the ones place?

____ ____ ____ ____ ____

2. Fill in the missing even numbers in each row.

10 ____ ____ ____   16 ____ ____ ____   22 ____ ____ ____

32 ____ ____ ____   38 ____ ____ ____   46 ____ ____ ____

60 ____ ____ ____   68 ____ ____ ____   74 ____ ____ ____

3. What even number comes next?

34 ____   16 ____   28 ____

42 ____   8 ____   48 ____

54 ____   62 ____   76 ____

4. What even number comes before?

____ 14   ____ 26   ____ 32

____ 6   ____ 20   ____ 40

____ 52   ____ 60   ____ 88

5. Write three even numbers over 100.

____ ____ ____

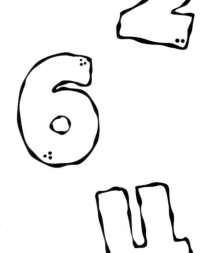

Name _____   Date _____

Odd Numbers

Directions:

Starting at 1, count by 2s to count the **odd** numbers. Lightly shade each number you count.

0	1	2	3	4	5	6	7	8	9
10	11	12	13	14	15	16	17	18	19
20	21	22	23	24	25	26	27	28	29
30	31	32	33	34	35	36	37	38	39
40	41	42	43	44	45	46	47	48	49

1. What numbers do the odd numbers have in the ones place?

____ ____ ____ ____ ____

2. Fill in the missing odd numbers in each row.

11 ___ ___   17 ___ ___   23 ___ ___ ___

35 ___ ___   41 ___ ___   47 ___ ___ ___

75 ___ ___   81 ___ ___   89 ___ ___

3. What odd number comes next?

7 ___   13 ___   25 ___

31 ___   47 ___   49 ___

53 ___   61 ___   75 ___

4. What odd number comes before?

___ 5   ___ 17   ___ 23

___ 31   ___ 45   ___ 49

___ 57   ___ 83   ___ 95

5. Write three odd numbers over 100.

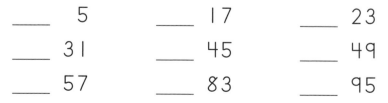

____ ____ ____

Name _____ Date _____

Counting Corners in Triangles

Directions:
Count the corners in the triangles. Write the numbers inside the shapes. Then, use the number pattern in the triangles to help answer the questions below.

1. How many corners do 4 triangles have? _____

2. How many corners do 8 triangles have? _____

3. How many corners do 10 triangles have? _____

4. How many corners do 11 triangles have? _____

5. How many triangles do 6 corners make? _____

6. How many triangles do 15 corners make? _____

7. How many triangles do 30 corners make? _____

8. How many triangles do 36 corners make? _____

Triangle Toughies

9. How many corners do 50 triangles have? _____

10. How many triangles do 300 corners make? _____

Name _____ Date _____

Skip Counting

Directions:

Count the corners in the squares. Write the numbers inside the shapes. Then, use the number pattern in the squares to help answer the questions below.

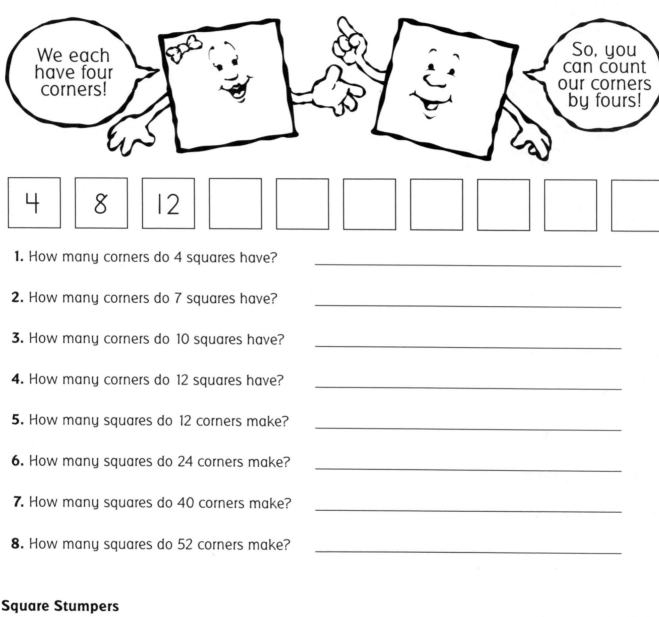

1. How many corners do 4 squares have? _____

2. How many corners do 7 squares have? _____

3. How many corners do 10 squares have? _____

4. How many corners do 12 squares have? _____

5. How many squares do 12 corners make? _____

6. How many squares do 24 corners make? _____

7. How many squares do 40 corners make? _____

8. How many squares do 52 corners make? _____

Square Stumpers

9. How many corners do 30 squares have? _____

10. How many squares do 100 corners make? _____

Name _____   Date _____

Counting Corners in Pentagons

Directions:

Count the corners in the pentagons. Write the numbers inside the shapes. Then, use the number pattern in the pentagons to help answer the questions below.

1. How many corners do 5 pentagons have?   _____

2. How many corners do 8 pentagons have?   _____

3. How many corners do 10 pentagons have?   _____

4. How many corners do 13 pentagons have?   _____

5. How many pentagons do 20 corners make?   _____

6. How many pentagons do 35 corners make?   _____

7. How many pentagons do 50 corners make?   _____

8. How many pentagons do 70 corners make?   _____

Pentagon Puzzlers

9. How many corners do 20 pentagons have?   _____

10. How many pentagons do 150 corners make?   _____

Counting Corners in Hexagons

Directions:

Count the corners in the hexagons. Write the numbers inside the shapes. Then, use the number pattern in the hexagons to help answer the questions below.

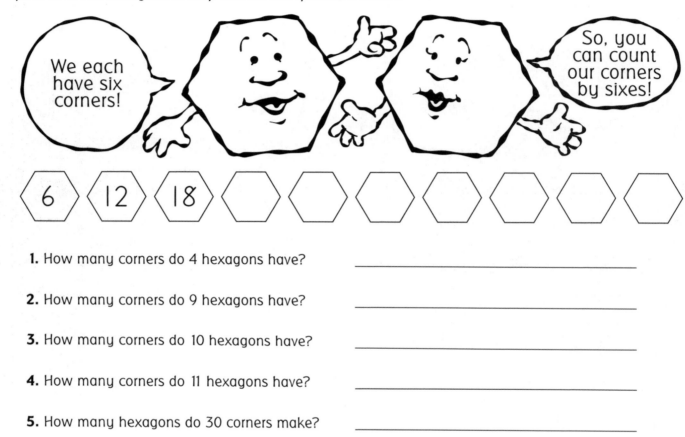

1. How many corners do 4 hexagons have?   _____

2. How many corners do 9 hexagons have?   _____

3. How many corners do 10 hexagons have?   _____

4. How many corners do 11 hexagons have?   _____

5. How many hexagons do 30 corners make?   _____

6. How many hexagons do 48 corners make?   _____

7. How many hexagons do 60 corners make?   _____

8. How many hexagons do 72 corners make?   _____

Hexagon Hurdles

9. How many corners do 20 hexagons have?   _____

10. How many hexagons do 600 corners make?   _____

Name _____   Date _____

Five and Ten Cent Stories

Directions:
Count the nickels or dimes to tell how much money each person has.

1.	Nick's money

_____ ¢

2.	Nancy's money

_____ ¢

3.	Nita's money

_____ ¢

4.	Dion's money

_____ ¢

5.	Diamond's money

_____ ¢

6.	Diane's money

_____ ¢

7. Who has the most money? _____

8. Who has the least money? _____

9. Which two people have the same amount of money?

_____   _____

Name _____   **Date** _____

Neat Number Patterns

Skip Counting

Directions:
Skip count to continue each pattern. Do not repeat.

1. | 2 | 4 | 6 | 8 | | | | | | | | | | |

2. | 1 | 3 | 5 | 7 | | | | | | | | | | |

3. | 3 | 6 | 9 | 12 | | | | | | | | | | |

4. | 5 | 10 | 15 | 20 | | | | | | | | | | |

5. | 10 | 20 | 30 | 40 | | | | | | | | | | |

6. | 4 | 8 | 12 | 16 | | | | | | | | | | |

7. | 6 | 12 | 18 | 24 | | | | | | | | | | |

8. | 50 | 52 | 54 | 56 | | | | | | | | | | |

9. | 61 | 63 | 65 | 67 | | | | | | | | | | |

Name _____   Date _____

Number Rainbows

Directions:
Connect numbers written in rows to make rainbows. These rainbows will show you addition sentences. Look at the example. Then, make your own rainbows and write the addition sentences that go with them.

Example: The Four Rainbow

0   1   2   3   4

Number Sentences

$0 + 4 = 4$
$1 + 3 = 4$
$2 + 2 = 4$

1. **The Five Rainbow**

0   1   2   3   4   5

= 5

= 5

= 5

2. **The Six Rainbow**

0   1   2   3   4   5   6

= 6

= 6

= 6

= 6

3. **The Seven Rainbow**

0   1   2   3   4   5   6   7

= 7

= 7

= 7

= 7

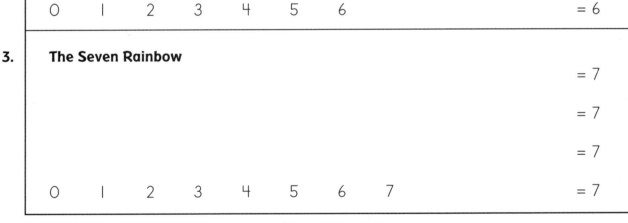

Elementary Algebra • CD-104104

More Number Rainbows

Addition Patterns

Directions:

Make rainbows for these numbers and write the addition sentences that go with them.

---

1. **The Eight Rainbow**

= 8

= 8

= 8

= 8

0   1   2   3   4   5   6   7   8

= 8

---

2. **The Nine Rainbow**

= 9

= 9

= 9

= 9

0   1   2   3   4   5   6   7   8   9

= 9

---

3. **The Ten Rainbow**

= 10

= 10

= 10

0   1   2   3   4   5   6   7   8   9   10

= 10

= 10

= 10

Change-o-Matic Machines

Functions

Directions:

Change-o-Matic machines change numbers in different ways. Look at each machine to see how it will change the number going in. Then, write the number that will come out.

Example:

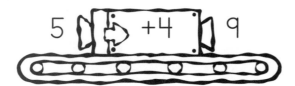

5 ⟹ +4   9

1.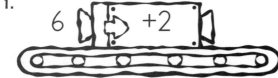

6 ⟹ +2

2.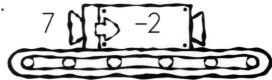

7 ⟹ -2

3.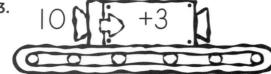

10 ⟹ +3

4.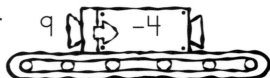

9 ⟹ -4

5.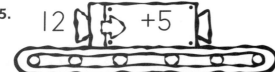

12 ⟹ +5

6.

5 ⟹ -5

7.

+1

7
15
20
39
52

8.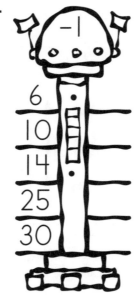

-1

6
10
14
25
30

9.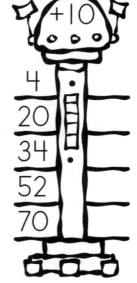

+10

4
20
34
52
70

More Change-o-Matic Machines

Functions

Directions:
Each machine has changed a number into another number. Work backward to find the starting number.

Example:

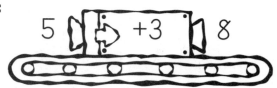

1.

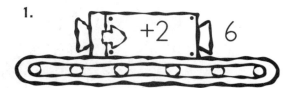

2.

3.

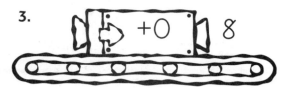

4.

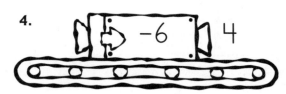

5.

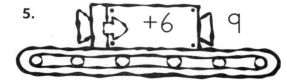

6.

7.

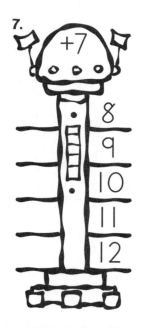

8.

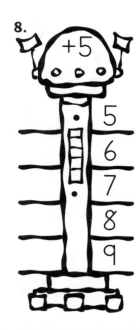

Name _____   Date _____

Directions:
Each machine has changed a number into another number. Figure out what each machine does and write it on the machine. Fill in the missing numbers on the machines.

Example:

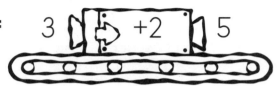

3 ⟹ +2 → 5

1.

5 ⟹ → 6

2.

4 ⟹ → 7

3.

9 ⟹ → 19

4.

7 ⟹ → 1

5.

8 ⟹ → 3

6.

15 ⟹ → 7

7.
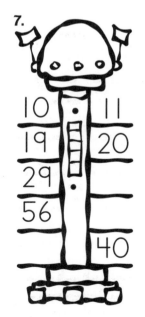

10	11
19	20
29	
56	
	40

8.
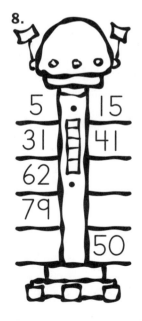

5	15
31	41
62	
79	
	50

9.
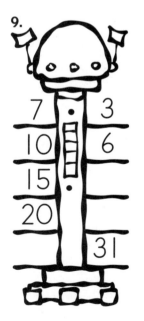

7	3
10	6
15	
20	
	31

Name _____   Date _____

Yummy Gummies

Directions:
The Dandy Candy Company sells gummy creatures. Gummy snakes cost 3¢ each. Gummy beetles cost 4¢ each. Fill in the charts below. Then, answer the questions.

Number of Gummy Snakes	Cost
1	3¢
2	6¢
3	
4	
5	
6	

Number of Gummy Beetles	Cost
1	4¢
2	8¢
3	
4	
5	
6	

1. Tell how much each would cost.

    3 gummy snakes _____   4 gummy beetles _____

    5 gummy snakes _____   6 gummy beetles _____

    7 gummy snakes _____   8 gummy beetles _____

    10 gummy snakes _____   10 gummy beetles _____

2. Which costs more?

    3 gummy snakes or 3 gummy beetles   _____

    5 gummy snakes or 4 gummy beetles   _____

    4 gummy snakes or 3 gummy beetles   _____

    6 gummy snakes or 4 gummy beetles   _____

3. How much would they cost together?

    3 gummy snakes and 3 gummy beetles   _____

    5 gummy snakes and 2 gummy beetles   _____

Name _____   Date _____

More Yummy Gummies

Directions:

The Dandy Candy Company also sells gummy frogs for 5¢ each and gummy turtles for 10¢ each. Fill in the charts below. Then, answer the questions.

Number of Gummy Frogs	Cost
1	5¢
2	
3	
4	
5	
6	

Number of Gummy Turtles	Cost
1	10¢
2	
3	
4	
5	
6	

1. If you have 20¢, how many gummy frogs can you buy? _____

   If you have 20¢, how many gummy turtles can you buy? _____

2. If you have 30¢, how many gummy frogs can you buy? _____

   If you have 30¢, how many gummy turtles can you buy? _____

3. How much would each cost?

   7 gummy frogs _____   7 gummy turtles _____

   10 gummy frogs _____   10 gummy turtles _____

4. Which costs less?

   3 gummy frogs or 3 gummy turtles   _____

   4 gummy frogs or 2 gummy turtles   _____

5. How much would they cost together?

   4 gummy frogs and 2 gummy turtles   _____

   5 gummy frogs and 5 gummy turtles   _____

Name _____   Date _____

Greater Than or Less Than?

Directions:
Follow the directions for each set of numbers.

1. Draw a triangle around the number that is equal to 7.
Circle the numbers that are less than 7.
Draw boxes around the numbers that are greater than 7.

0   1   2   3   4   5   6   7   8   9   10   11   12   13   14

2. Draw a triangle around the number that is equal to 25.
Circle the numbers that are less than 25.
Draw boxes around the numbers that are greater than 25.

19   20   21   22   23   24   25   26   27   28   29   30   31

3. Draw a triangle around the number that is equal to 30.
Circle the numbers that are less than 30.
Draw boxes around the numbers that are greater than 30.

27   28   29   30   31   32   33   34   35   36   37   38   39

4. Draw a triangle around the number that is equal to 46.
Circle the numbers that are less than 46.
Draw boxes around the numbers that are greater than 46.

38   39   40   41   42   43   44   45   46   47   48   49   50

Comparing Length

Equality & Inequality

Directions:

Circle the true number sentence in each box.

Example: Pencils P  E P < E P = E (P > E)	**1.** Markers M  A M < A M = A M > A
2. Brushes B 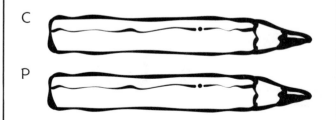 R B = R B > R B < R	**3.** Chalk C  H C > H C < H C = H
4. Colored Pencils C  P C = P C > P C < P	**5.** Erasers E  R E < R E = R E > R

Name _____   Date _____

Comparing Height

Directions:
Write a number sentence to tell which letter is taller. Keep the letters in order and use >, <, or = to write each statement.

Example: Z Y

_____ Z > Y _____

1.

_____

2.   V U

_____

3.

_____

4.   R Q

_____

5.

_____

6.

_____

7.   L K

_____

8.   J I

_____

9.

_____

10.

_____

11.   D C

_____

Name _____   Date _____

What Is True?

Directions:
Circle the true number sentences for each set of objects.

1. Bolts

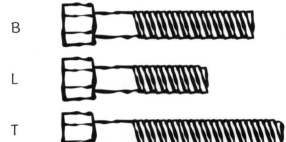

B

L

T

B < L   B = L   L > T   B < T   B > L   L < T   L = T

2. Screws

S

C

R

S > R   S = R   S < C   S < R   C > R   S = C   R > C

3. Nails

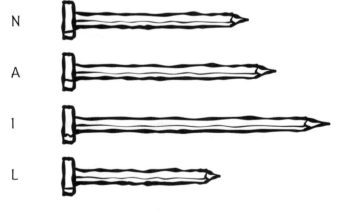

N

A

I

L

N > A   N > L   A > I   I > L   L < A   I < N   N = L

Name _____ Date _____

Number Riddles

Equality & Inequality

Directions:

Write the number in each box that answers the riddle.

1.

I am less than 10.
I am greater than 5.
I am not equal to 8.

What number am I? _____

2.

I am less than 15.
I am greater than 10.
I am not equal to 12.

What number am I? _____

3.

I am less than 6.
I am greater than 3.
I am not equal to 4.

What number am I? _____

4.

I am less than 20.
I am greater than 13.
I am not equal to 15.

What number am I? _____

5.

I am less than 30.
I am greater than 24.
I am not equal to 26.

What number am I? _____

6.

I am less than 40.
I am greater than 30.
I am not equal to 35.

What number am I? _____

Name _____   Date _____

Sharing Crackers

Fair Shares

Directions:

Jon and Donna shared some crackers. Some of the crackers are circles and some are squares. Look at the sets below, then answer the questions.

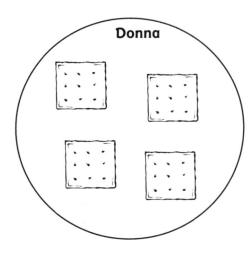

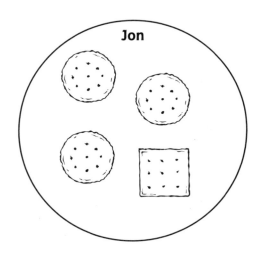

1. How many square crackers does Donna have? _____

2. How many square crackers does Jon have? _____

3. How many circle crackers does Jon have? _____

4. How many crackers does Jon have altogether? _____

5. Do Jon and Donna have the same number of crackers? _____

6. What is another way to write how many crackers Jon has? _____ + _____

7. Circle the number sentences below that tell something true about Jon and Donna's crackers.

$4 = 4$ $4 > 4$ $4 = 3 + 1$

$4 = 1 + 3$ $4 = 3 + 3$ $3 + 1 = 4$

Name _____   Date _____

Sharing More Crackers   **Fair Shares**

Directions:

Amy and Jamal shared some crackers. Some of the crackers are circles and some are squares. Look at the sets below, then answer the questions.

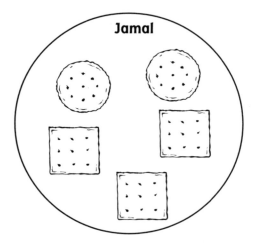

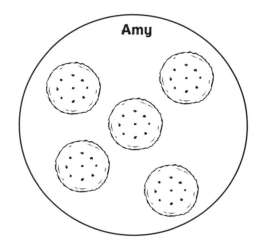

1. How many square crackers does Jamal have?   _____

2. How many circle crackers does Jamal have?   _____

3. How many crackers does Jamal have altogether?   _____

4. How many circle crackers does Amy have?   _____

5. Do Amy and Jamal have the same number of crackers?   _____

6. What is another way to write how many crackers Jamal has?   _____ + _____

7. Circle the number sentences below that tell something true about Amy and Jamal's crackers.

$5 > 5$ $5 = 5$ $3 + 2 = 5$

$3 - 2 = 5$ $2 + 3 = 5$ $5 + 5 = 5$

Name _____   Date _____

Sharing Cookies

Directions:
Susan and Ashley shared some cookies. Some of the cookies are circles, some are triangles, and some are squares. Look at the sets below, then answer the questions.

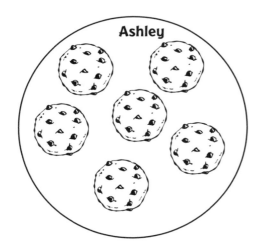

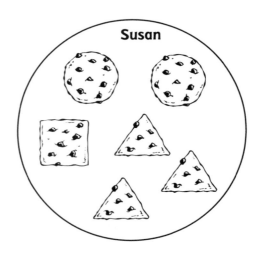

1. How many circle cookies does Ashley have? _____

2. How many circle cookies does Susan have? _____

3. How many triangle cookies does Susan have? _____

4. How many square cookies does Susan have? _____

5. How many cookies does Susan have altogether?_____

6. Do Susan and Ashley have the same number of cookies? _____

7. What is another way to write how many cookies Susan has? _____ + _____ + _____

8. Circle the number sentences below that tell something true about Ashley and Susan's cookies.

$6 = 6$ $6 < 6$ $6 = 2 + 3 + 1$

$6 = 2 + 3$ $6 = 3 + 1 + 2$ $6 + 3 = 1 + 2$

Sharing More Cookies

Fair Shares

Directions:

Kelly and Enrique shared some cookies. Some of the cookies are circles, some are triangles, and some are squares. Look at the sets below, then answer the questions.

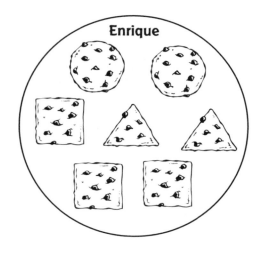

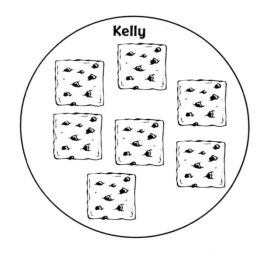

1. How many circle cookies does Enrique have? _____

2. How many triangle cookies does Enrique have? _____

3. How many square cookies does Enrique have? _____

4. How many cookies does Enrique have altogether? _____

5. How many square cookies does Kelly have? _____

6. Do Kelly and Enrique have the same number of cookies? _____

7. What is another way to write how many cookies Enrique has? _____ + _____ + _____

8. Circle the number sentences below that tell something true about Kelly and Enrique's cookies.

$7 = 7$ $7 > 7$ $6 = 7$

$2 + 2 + 3 = 7$ $2 + 2 = 7 + 3$ $2 + 3 + 2 = 7$

Name _____ Date _____

Directions:
Jen and Myong shared some fruit. They have bananas and apples. Look at the sets below, then answer the questions.

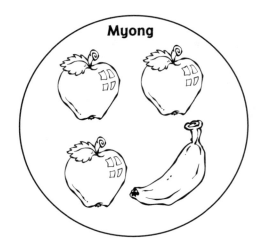

1. How many apples does Myong have? _____

2. How many bananas does Myong have? _____

3. How many pieces of fruit does Myong have altogether? _____

4. What is another way to write how much fruit Myong has? _____ + _____

5. How many apples does Jen have? _____

6. How many bananas does Jen have? _____

7. How many pieces of fruit does Jen have altogether? _____

8. What is another way to write how much fruit Jen has? _____ + _____

9. Do Jen and Myong have fair shares? _____

10. Circle the number sentences that tell something true about Jen and Myong's fruit.

$4 = 4$ $3 > 4$ $4 = 2 + 2$

$3 + 1 = 4$ $3 + 1 = 2$ $3 + 1 = 2 + 2$

Drawing Fair Shares

⭐ **Fair Shares**

Directions:

The number sentences in each box tell about fair shares. Draw pictures to show the fair shares. Use circles and squares.

Example: me you 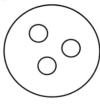 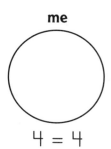 3 = 3 3 = 1 + 2	**1.** me you 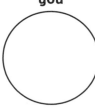 4 = 4 3 + 1 = 4
2. me you 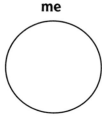 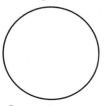 2 = 2 2 = 1 + 1	**3.** me you 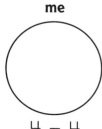  4 = 4 2 + 2 = 4
4. me you 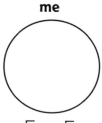 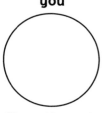 5 = 5 5 = 4 + 1	**5.** me you 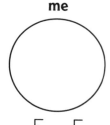 5 = 5 3 + 2 = 5
6. me you 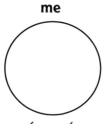 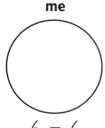 6 = 6 6 = 5 + 1	**7.** me you 6 = 6 2 + 4 = 6

Name _____ Date _____

Writing about Fair Shares

 **Fair Shares**

Directions:
Write two number sentences to tell about the fair shares in each box.

Example: me   you

$3 = 3$ $3 = 2 + 1$
_____   _____

1. me   you

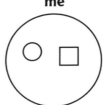 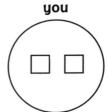

_____   _____

2. me   you

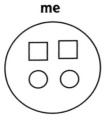

_____   _____

3. me   you

_____   _____

4. me   you

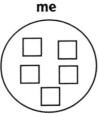 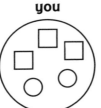

_____   _____

5. me   you

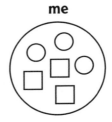 

_____   _____

6. me   you

_____   _____

7. me   you

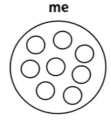 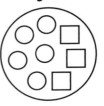

_____   _____

More Writing about Fair Shares

Fair Shares

Directions:
Write one number sentence to tell about the fair shares in each box.

Example: me   you

$$3 + 1 = 2 + 2$$
_____

1.   me   you

_____

2.   me   you

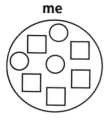
_____

3.   me   you

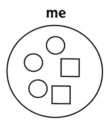
_____

4.   me   you

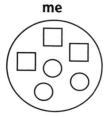
_____

5.   me   you

_____

6.   me   you

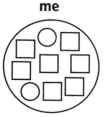
_____

7.   me   you

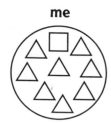
_____

Name _____   Date _____

Directions:
Carrie and Jeff have some oranges. Look at the sets below, then answer the questions.

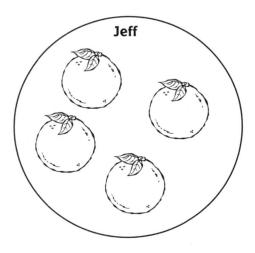

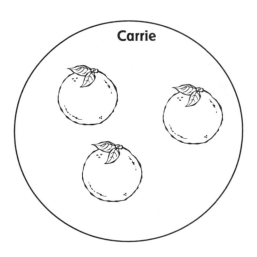

1. How many oranges does Jeff have? _____

2. How many oranges does Carrie have? _____

3. Do Carrie and Jeff have fair shares? _____

4. Do Carrie and Jeff have unfair shares? _____

5. Write a number sentence about their shares. _____ > _____

6. Add to Carrie's oranges so that they have fair shares. How many oranges did you add? _____

7. Do they have fair shares now? _____

8. Write a number sentence that tells what you did to make the shares fair.

_____ = _____

Name _____   Date _____

Sharing Blocks

Directions:

Michelle and Richard have some blocks. Look at the sets below, then answer the questions.

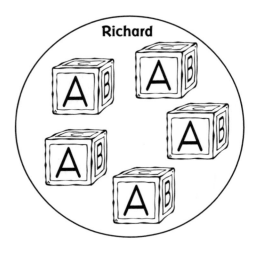

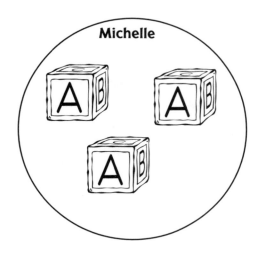

1. How many blocks does Richard have? _____

2. How many blocks does Michelle have? _____

3. Do they have fair shares? _____

4. Do they have unfair shares? _____

5. Write a number sentence about their shares.   _____ > _____

6. Cross out some of Richard's blocks so that they have fair shares. How many blocks did you subtract?

_____

7. Do they have fair shares now? _____

8. Write a number sentence that tells what you did to make the shares fair.

_____ = _____

Name _____   Date _____

Sharing Brownies

Directions:
Pam and Bill have some brownies. Look at the sets below, then answer the questions.

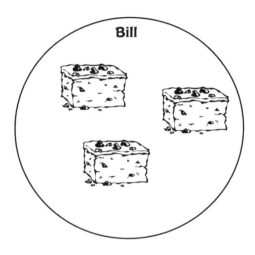

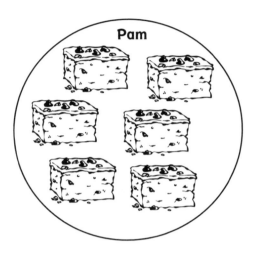

1. How many brownies does Bill have? _____

2. How many brownies does Pam have? _____

3. Do they have fair shares? _____

4. Do they have unfair shares? _____

5. Write a number sentence about their shares.   _____ < _____

6. Add to Bill's brownies so that they have fair shares. How many brownies did you add? _____

7. Do they have fair shares now? _____

8. Write a number sentence that tells what you did to make the shares fair.

_____ = _____

Name _____   Date _____

Unfair Shares

Directions:

Julie and Ray have some peanuts. Look at the sets below, then answer the questions.

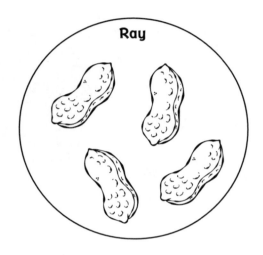

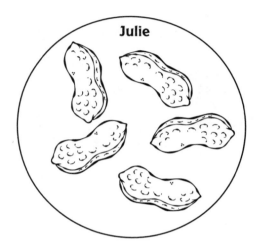

1. How many peanuts does Julie have? _____

2. How many peanuts does Ray have? _____

3. Do they have fair shares? _____

4. Do they have unfair shares? _____

5. Write a number sentence about their shares. _____ < _____

6. Cross out some of Julie's peanuts so that they have fair shares. How many peanuts did you subtract?

_____

7. Do they have fair shares now? _____

8. Write a number sentence that tells what you did to make the shares fair.

_____ = _____

Name _____   Date _____

Making Shares Fair

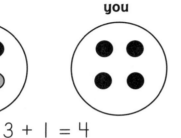 Unfair Shares

Directions:

Make the shares in each box fair by adding or subtracting. Then, write a number sentence to tell what you did.

Example: me you  Add. $3 + 1 = 4$	**1.** me you 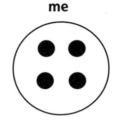  Add. _____
2. me you 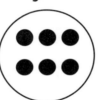 Subtract. _____	**3.** me you 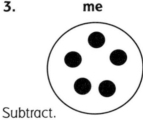  Subtract. _____
4. me you 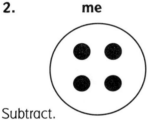 Add. _____	**5.** me you 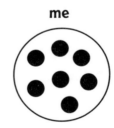  Add. _____
6. me you  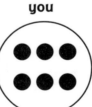 Subtract. _____	**7.** me you 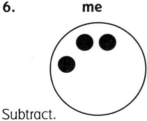 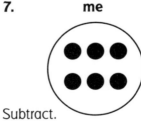 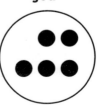 Subtract. _____

Balancing Numbers

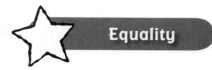

Equality

Directions:

Look at the numbers on the ends of each balance. Should they be balanced? Circle yes or no.

Example:

yes (no)   because 4 + 2 = 6, not 7

1.

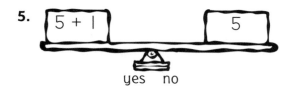

yes   no

2.

yes   no

3.

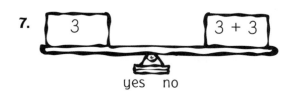

yes   no

4.

yes   no

5.

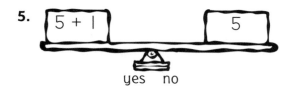

yes   no

6.

yes   no

7.

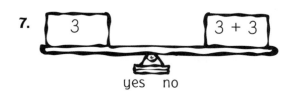

yes   no

8.

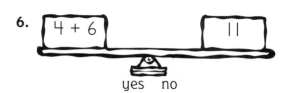

yes   no

9.

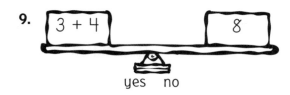

yes   no

10.

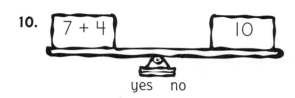

yes   no

11.

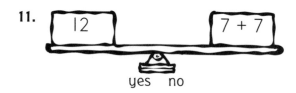

yes   no

12.

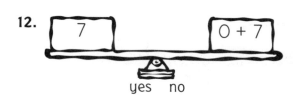

yes   no

Name _____   Date _____

Balancing More Numbers

Directions:

Look at the numbers on the ends of each balance. Should they be balanced? Circle yes or no.

Example:

yes   no   because 3 + 3 = 6 and 2 + 4 = 6

1.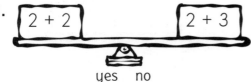

yes   no

2.

yes   no

3.

yes   no

4.

yes   no

5.

yes   no

6.

yes   no

7.

yes   no

8.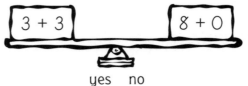

yes   no

9.

yes   no

10.

yes   no

11.

yes   no

12.

yes   no

Equal Addition Bugs

Equality

Directions:
Circle the two bugs in each box with equal sums. Write a number sentence to show they are equal.

1.
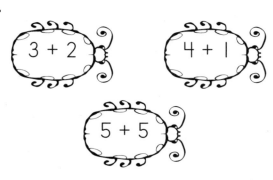

_____ = _____

2.

_____ = _____

3.
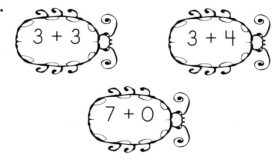

_____ = _____

4.
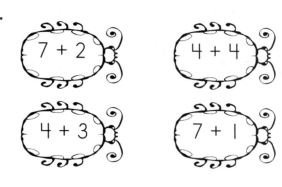

_____ = _____

5.
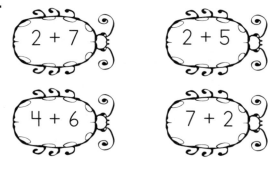

_____ = _____

6.
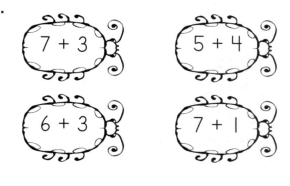

_____ = _____

     Elementary Algebra • CD-104104

Name _____ Date _____

Equal Subtraction Bugs

Directions:

Circle the two bugs in each box with equal differences. Write a number sentence to show they are equal.

1.

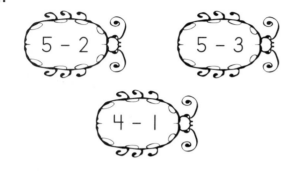

_____ = _____

2.

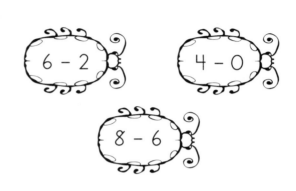

_____ = _____

3.

_____ = _____

4.

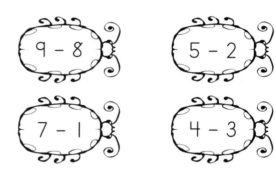

_____ = _____

5.

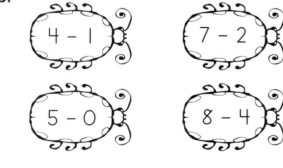

_____ = _____

6.

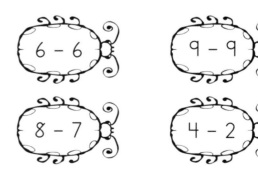

_____ = _____

Mixed Equal Bugs

Equality

Directions:

Circle the two bugs in each box with equal answers. Write a number sentence to show they are equal.

1.

2 + 2   7 – 3

4 + 1   5 – 2

_____ = _____

2.

8 – 5   5 + 3

2 + 1   6 – 4

_____ = _____

3.

1 + 1   7 – 5

6 – 3   3 + 4

_____ = _____

4.

7 – 2   4 + 4

5 + 3   8 – 1

_____ = _____

5.

5 + 2   8 – 6

6 – 3

2 – 0   2 + 2

_____ = _____

6.

2 + 3   9 – 4

6 + 1

1 + 5   5 – 1

_____ = _____

Elementary Algebra • CD-104104

Find the Plus Partners

★ Equality

Directions:
Cut out all of the boxes on the right of the page. Glue the boxes in the spaces to make true number sentences.

1. [ ] = [ ]

2. [ ] = [ ]

3. [ ] = [ ]

4. [ ] = [ ]

5. [ ] = [ ]

6. [ ] = [ ]

7 + 0	3 + 6	4 + 3
5 + 1	4 + 4	3 + 3
2 + 3	5 + 4	3 + 2
3 + 1	6 + 2	2 + 2

Find the Minus Partners

Equality

Directions:

Cut out all of the boxes on the right of the page. Glue the boxes in the spaces to make true number sentences.

1. ☐ = ☐

2. ☐ = ☐

3. ☐ = ☐

4. ☐ = ☐

5. ☐ = ☐

6. ☐ = ☐

7 - 2	6 - 2	7 - 4
4 - 0	4 - 2	3 - 1
6 - 3	6 - 1	7 - 1
3 - 2	10 - 4	5 - 4

Find the Mixed Partners

Equality

Directions:
Cut out all of the boxes on the right of the page. Glue the boxes in the spaces to make true number sentences.

1. [ ] = [ ]

2. [ ] = [ ]

3. [ ] = [ ]

4. [ ] = [ ]

5. [ ] = [ ]

6. [ ] = [ ]

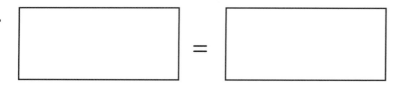

$6 + 1$	$4 + 4$	$7 - 2$
$2 + 2$	$5 - 1$	$9 - 2$
$3 + 2$	$6 - 3$	$7 - 1$
$2 + 1$	$3 + 3$	$10 - 2$

Equal Schmequal

Equality

This is a game for 2 players.

Directions:
1. Cut out the playing cards below and the scorecards on page 63.
2. Turn the playing cards upside down and mix them up.
3. Take turns drawing one card at a time.
4. If you have two cards with equal amounts, put them in two of the boxes on your scorecard. If you have two cards with unequal amounts, place the cards facedown in their original positions.
5. The first player to fill up all of the boxes on her scorecard wins.

4	5	5 + 4	7 – 1
4 + 4	2 + 2	10 – 1	8
3 + 3	9 – 1	5 + 2	5 – 1
3 + 1	6	7 – 2	3 + 6
4 + 3	7	2 + 3	9
1 + 4	2 + 6	9 – 2	6 + 0

                   Elementary Algebra • CD-104104

Name _____   Date _____

Equal Schmequal Scorecards

Equality

_____**'s Equal Schmequal Scorecard**

   **=**

   **=**

_____**'s Equal Schmequal Scorecard**

   **=**

   **=**

   **=**

Make an Addition Design

Directions:

Find two pairs of numbers that are equal. Then, connect their dots with a straight line. Write the number pairs together in a complete number sentence on a line below. The first one has been done for you. Repeat until all of the equal pairs of numbers have been found. Color your design.

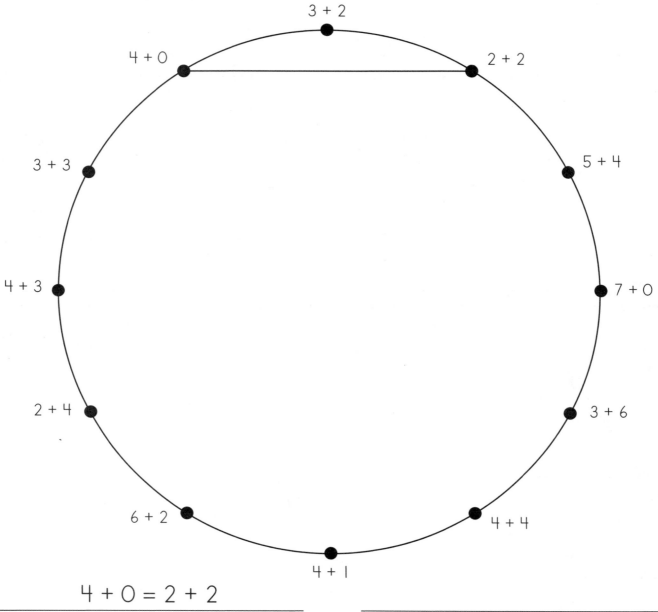

$4 + 0 = 2 + 2$

_____   _____

_____   _____

_____   _____

Make a Subtraction Design

Directions:

Find two pairs of numbers that are equal. Then, connect their dots with a straight line. Write the number pairs together in a complete number sentence on a line below. Repeat until all of the equal pairs of numbers have been found. Color your design.

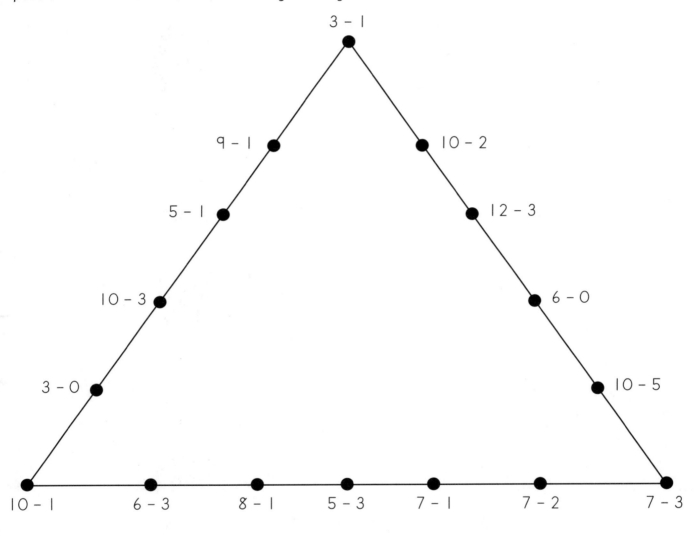

_____   _____

_____   _____

_____   _____

_____   _____

Name _____   Date _____

Make a Mixed Design

Equality

Directions:
Find two pairs of numbers that are equal. Then, connect their dots with a straight line. Write the number pairs together in a complete number sentence on a line below. Repeat until all of the equal pairs of numbers have been found. Color your design.

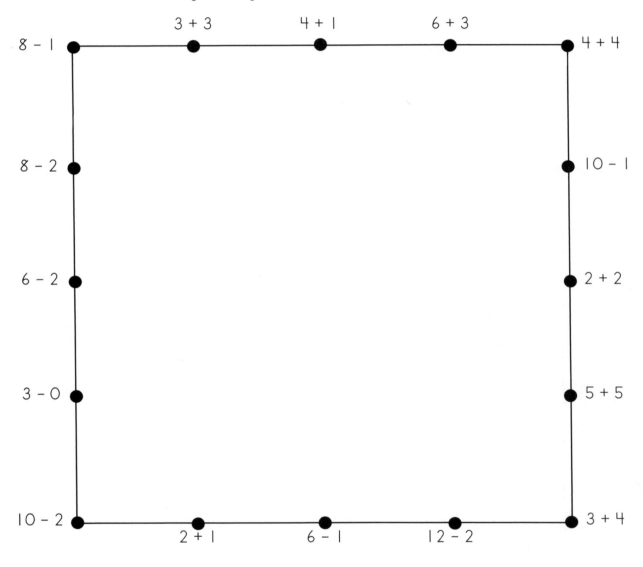

8 − 1   3 + 3   4 + 1   6 + 3   4 + 4

8 − 2   10 − 1

6 − 2   2 + 2

3 − 0   5 + 5

10 − 2   2 + 1   6 − 1   12 − 2   3 + 4

_____   _____

_____   _____

_____   _____

_____   _____

Make Another Mixed Design

Equality

Directions:

Find two pairs of numbers that are equal. Then, connect their dots with a straight line. Write the number pairs together in a complete number sentence on a line below. Repeat until all of the equal pairs of numbers have been found. Color your design.

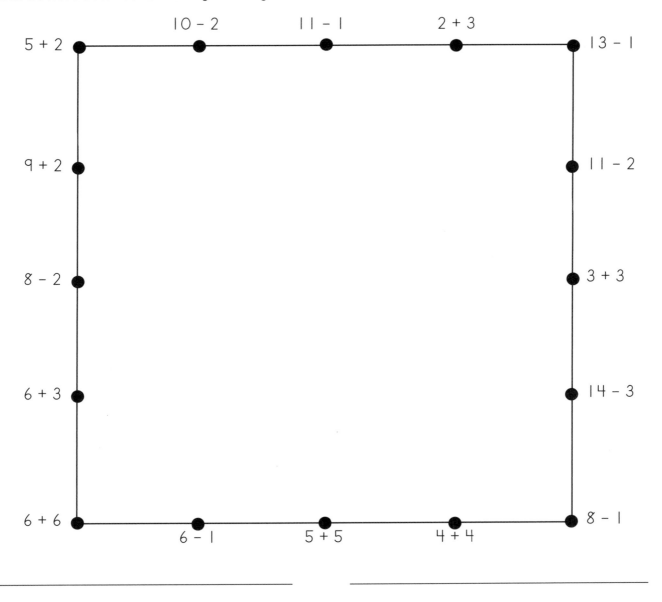

_____   _____

_____   _____

_____   _____

_____   _____

What Is True?

Directions:

Circle all of the number sentences below that are true. Then, answer the questions.

$7 = 7$ $8 > 7$

$7 = 8$ $8 < 7$

$4 + 3 = 7$ $7 = 4 + 3$

$4 + 4 = 7$ $7 = 4 + 4$

$7 + 4 = 3$ $7 = 3 + 4$

$4 + 3 = 4 + 3$ $4 + 3 = 3 + 4$

$4 + 3 = 4 + 4$ $4 + 3 = 1$

1. Why is $4 + 3 = 3 + 4$ true?

_____

_____

2. Why is $4 + 3 = 4 + 4$ not true?

_____

_____

What Else Is True?

Directions:
Circle all of the number sentences below that are true. Then, answer the questions.

$9 = 9$

$8 = 9$

$9 > 8$

$1 > 9$

$8 + 1 = 9$

$9 - 8 = 1$

$1 = 8 - 9$

$9 = 8 + 1$

$8 = 9 - 1$

$9 = 1 + 8$

$8 - 1 = 9$

$8 - 9 = 1$

$8 + 1 = 10 - 1$

$9 - 8 = 9 - 1$

$9 + 1 = 8 - 1$

$9 - 8 = 8 - 9$

1. Why is 8 + 1 = 10 - 1 true?

_____

_____

2. Why is 9 - 8 = 8 - 9 not true?

_____

_____

3. Why is 9 + 1 = 8 - 1 not true?

_____

_____

Name _____   Date _____

You Make It True

Directions:
Use any numbers to make these number sentences true.

1. _____ = 3

2. _____ > 4

3. _____ = 5

4. _____ < 9

5. 7 = _____

6. 7 > _____

7. 10 = _____

8. 8 < _____

9. _____ + _____ = 6

10. 8 = _____ + _____

11. _____ + _____ = 4

12. 5 = _____ + _____

13. _____ + 1 = _____

14. _____ = 6 + _____

15. _____ + 3 = _____

16. _____ = 2 + _____

17. 5 + _____ = _____

18. _____ = _____ + 3

19. 4 + _____ = _____

20. _____ = _____ + 1

21. _____ + _____ + _____ = 7

22. 9 = _____ + _____ + _____

Name _____   Date _____

You Make It True

Directions:

Use any numbers and operation signs to make these number sentences true.

1. _____ = 4

2. _____ < 10

3. _____ = 100

4. _____ > 12

5. 20 = _____

6. 6 > _____

7. 1 = _____

8. 9 < _____

9. _____ − _____ = 3

10. 4 = _____ − _____

11. _____ − _____ = 1

12. 5 = _____ − _____

13. 7 − _____ = _____

14. _____ = 6 − _____

15. 5 − _____ = _____

16. _____ = 4 − _____

17. _____ − 2 = _____

18. _____ = _____ − 3

19. _____ − 0 = _____

20. _____ = _____ − 1

21. _____ − _____ = 2

22. 10 = _____ − _____

Name _____   Date _____

You Make It True

Directions:
Use any numbers to make these number sentences true.

1. _____ + 2 = _____

2. 6 − _____ = _____

3. _____ + 3 = _____

4. 10 − _____ = _____

5. 6 + _____ = _____

6. _____ − _____ = 3

7. 4 + _____ = _____

8. _____ − _____ = 5

9. _____ + _____ = 8

10. _____ − 2 = _____

11. _____ + _____ = 5

12. _____ − 4 = _____

13. _____ = 5 + _____

14. _____ = 5 − _____

15. _____ = 1 + _____

16. _____ = 8 − _____

17. _____ = _____ + 7

18. 7 = _____ − _____

19. _____ = _____ + 8

20. 4 = _____ − _____

21. 6 = _____ + _____

22. _____ = _____ − 4

23. 4 = _____ + _____

24. _____ = _____ − 1

Name _____   **Date** _____

Eight Is Great

Directions:
Write number sentences with the sum of 8. Make each number sentence different. Use the circles below or count objects to help you.

1. $8 =$ _____ + _____

2. $8 =$ _____ + _____

3. $8 =$ _____ + _____

4. $8 =$ _____ + _____

5. $8 =$ _____ + _____

6. $8 =$ _____ + _____

7. $8 =$ _____ + _____

8. $8 =$ _____ + _____

9. $8 =$ _____ + _____

Now, try these without using zero. Make each number sentence different.

10. $8 =$ _____ + _____ + _____

11. $8 =$ _____ + _____ + _____

12. $8 =$ _____ + _____ + _____

13. $8 =$ _____ + _____ + _____

Try these bonus problems. Do not use zero.

14. $8 =$ _____ + _____ + _____ + _____

15. $8 =$ _____ + _____ + _____ + _____ + _____

16. $8 =$ _____ + _____ + _____ + _____ + _____ + _____

Nine Is Divine

Directions:
Write number sentences with the sum of 9. Make each number sentence different. Use the circles below or count objects to help you.

1. 9 = _____ + _____

2. 9 = _____ + _____

3. 9 = _____ + _____

4. 9 = _____ + _____

5. 9 = _____ + _____

6. 9 = _____ + _____

7. 9 = _____ + _____

8. 9 = _____ + _____

9. 9 = _____ + _____

10. 9 = _____ + _____

Now, try these without using zero. Make each number sentence different.

11. 9 = _____ + _____ + _____

12. 9 = _____ + _____ + _____

13. 9 = _____ + _____ + _____

14. 9 = _____ + _____ + _____

Try these bonus problems. Do not use zero.

15. 9 = _____ + _____ + _____ + _____

16. 9 = _____ + _____ + _____ + _____ + _____

17. 9 = _____ + _____ + _____ + _____ + _____ + _____

Name _____   Date _____

Ten Is Terrific

Directions:

Write number sentences with the sum of 10. Make each number sentence different. Use the circles below or count objects to help you.

1. $10 =$ _____ + _____

2. $10 =$ _____ + _____

3. $10 =$ _____ + _____

4. $10 =$ _____ + _____

5. $10 =$ _____ + _____

6. $10 =$ _____ + _____

7. $10 =$ _____ + _____

8. $10 =$ _____ + _____

9. $10 =$ _____ + _____

10. $10 =$ _____ + _____

11. $10 =$ _____ + _____

Now, try these without using zero. Make each number sentence different.

12. $10 =$ _____ + _____ + _____

13. $10 =$ _____ + _____ + _____

14. $10 =$ _____ + _____ + _____

15. $10 =$ _____ + _____ + _____

Try these bonus problems. Do not use zero.

16. $10 =$ _____ + _____ + _____ + _____

17. $10 =$ _____ + _____ + _____ + _____ + _____

18. $10 =$ _____ + _____ + _____ + _____ + _____ + _____

Eleven Is Heaven

Directions:

Write number sentences with the sum of 11. Make each number sentence different. Use the circles below or count objects to help you.

1. 11 = _____ + _____

2. 11 = _____ + _____

3. 11 = _____ + _____

4. 11 = _____ + _____

5. 11 = _____ + _____

6. 11 = _____ + _____

7. 11 = _____ + _____

8. 11 = _____ + _____

9. 11 = _____ + _____

10. 11 = _____ + _____

11. 11 = _____ + _____

12. 11 = _____ + _____

Now, try these without using zero. Make each number sentence different.

13. 11 = _____ + _____ + _____

14. 11 = _____ + _____ + _____

15. 11 = _____ + _____ + _____

16. 11 = _____ + _____ + _____

Try these bonus problems. Do not use zero.

17. 11 = _____ + _____ + _____ + _____

18. 11 = _____ + _____ + _____ + _____ + _____

19. 11 = _____ + _____ + _____ + _____ + _____ + _____

Twelve is Tremendous

Directions:
Write number sentences with the sum of 12. Make each number sentence different. Use the circles below or count objects to help you.

1. 12 = _____ + _____

2. 12 = _____ + _____

3. 12 = _____ + _____

4. 12 = _____ + _____

5. 12 = _____ + _____

6. 12 = _____ + _____

7. 12 = _____ + _____

8. 12 = _____ + _____

9. 12 = _____ + _____

10. 12 = _____ + _____

11. 12 = _____ + _____

12. 12 = _____ + _____

13. 12 = _____ + _____

Now, try these without using zero. Make each number sentence different.

14. 12 = _____ + _____ + _____

15. 12 = _____ + _____ + _____

16. 12 = _____ + _____ + _____

17. 12 = _____ + _____ + _____

Try these bonus problems. Do not use zero.

18. 12 = _____ + _____ + _____ + _____

19. 12 = _____ + _____ + _____ + _____ + _____

20. 12 = _____ + _____ + _____ + _____ + _____ + _____

Balloon Stories

Directions:
For each story, draw a picture and write a number sentence.

Example:
Ted had 3 balloons.
His mom got him 2 more.
Now, he has 5 balloons.

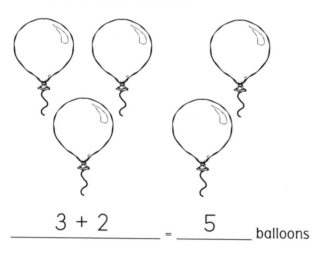

___3 + 2___ = __5__ balloons

1. Toya had 4 balloons.
She blew up 3 more.
Now, she has 7 balloons.

_____ = _____ balloons

2. Rex had 2 balloons.
His sister gave him 4 more.
Now, he has 6 balloons.

3. Rita had 1 balloon.
Her dad gave her 7 more.
Now, she has 8 balloons.

_____ = _____ balloons

_____ = _____ balloons

Name _____   Date _____

Book Stories

Directions:

For each story, draw a picture and write a number sentence.

Example:
Belle had 6 cat books.
She gave 2 to her friend.
Now, she has 4 books.

1. Tyler had 5 truck books.
He lost 1 on a trip.
Now, he has 4 books.

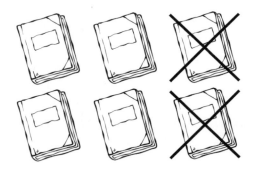

_____ 6 − 2 _____ = __ 4 __ books   _____ = _____ books

2. Tasha had 7 joke books.
She gave 4 to her brother.
Now, she has 3 books.

3. Darnell had 8 insect books.
His dog chewed up 3.
Now, he has 5 books.

_____ = _____ books   _____ = _____ books

Ball Stories

Directions:

For each story, draw a picture and write a number sentence.

1. Kelly had 3 table tennis balls.
She found 5 more.
Now, she has 8 table tennis balls.

2. Rico had 7 tennis balls.
He lost 2 of them.
Now, he has 5 tennis balls.

_____ = _____ table tennis balls

_____ = _____ tennis balls

3. Lonny had 6 baseballs.
He gave 3 of them to his friend.
Now, he has 3 baseballs.

4. Jane had 5 footballs.
She bought 2 more at the store.
Now, she has 7 footballs.

_____ = _____ baseballs

_____ = _____ footballs

5. Barbara had 8 rubber balls.
Her sister took 2 of them.
Now, she has 6 rubber balls.

6. Mike had 2 kick balls.
His father gave him 2 more.
Now, he has 4 kick balls.

_____ = _____ rubber balls

_____ = _____ kick balls

Name _____   Date _____

Write Your Own Math Stories

Directions:
For each number sentence, write a story about different colored markers.

Example:
3 + 2 = 5   I had 3 purple markers. My friend gave me 2 more. Now, I have 5 purple markers.

1. 4 + 2 = 6   _____

    _____

    _____

2. 5 − 4 = 1   _____

    _____

    _____

3. 5 + 4 = 9   _____

    _____

    _____

4. 6 − 3 = 3   _____

    _____

    _____

Name _____   Date _____

Families of Fruit

Directions:
Draw a picture to solve each problem. Write the answer on the line.

Example:

Patty Pear has 5 sisters.
She also has 3 brothers.
How many sisters and brothers
does Patty have altogether?

___8___ sisters and brothers

1. Alfie Apple has 2 aunts.
He also has 4 uncles.
How many aunts and uncles
does Alfie have altogether?

_____ aunts and uncles

2. Ben Blueberry has 2 grandmas.
He also has 2 grandpas.
How many grandparents.
does Ben have altogether?

_____ grandparents

3. Lili Lemon has 3 boy cousins.
She also has 4 girl cousins.
How many cousins does
Lili have altogether?

_____ cousins

4. Katie Kiwi has 6 neighbors on the left.
She also has 3 neighbors on the right.
How many neighbors does Katie
have altogether?

_____ neighbors

5. Ollie Orange has 1 brother.
He also has 6 sisters.
How many brothers and sisters
does Ollie have altogether?

_____ brothers and sisters

Fruit Family Pets

Directions:
Draw a picture to solve each problem. Write the answer on the line.

Example:

Ron Raspberry had 6 pet beetles.
Then, 2 got lost.
How many beetles were left?

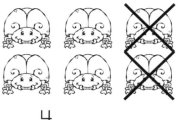

_____4_____ beetles

1. Lolly Lime had 5 pet flies.
Then, 1 flew away.
How many flies were left?

_____ flies

2. Bill Banana had 7 pet ants.
Then, 2 ran away.
How many ants were left?

_____ ants

3. Sally Strawberry had 8 pet butterflies.
Then, 4 fluttered away.
How many butterflies were left?

_____ butterflies

4. Greg Grapefruit had 9 pet bees.
Then, 2 went back to the hive.
How many bees were left?

_____ bees

5. Penny Peach had 7 pet caterpillars.
Then, 4 crawled away.
How many caterpillars were left?

_____ caterpillars

Fruit Friends' Clothing

Directions:
Draw a picture to solve each problem. Write the answer on the line.

1. Polly Plum had 6 T-shirts.
She got 2 more as a gift.
How many T-shirts does Polly
have now?

_____ T-shirts

2. Walt Watermelon had 8 baseball caps.
Then, 3 got dirty.
How many clean baseball caps
were left?

_____ clean baseball caps

3. Molly Mango had 6 soccer shirts.
Then, 3 got ripped.
How many soccer shirts did
Molly have left?

_____ soccer shirts

4. Cal Cranberry had 3 pairs of shorts.
His mom bought him 2 more pairs.
How many pairs of shorts does
Cal have now?

_____ pairs of shorts

5. Gina Grape had 5 sweatshirts.
She got 4 more for her birthday.
How many sweatshirts does
Gina have now?

_____ sweatshirts

6. David Date had 10 T-shirts.
He gave away 4 of them.
How many T-shirts does
David have left?

_____ T-shirts

Name _____   Date _____

Magic Show Math

Directions:
Draw a picture to solve each problem. Write a number sentence to show the answer.

Example:

Willy the Wonderful made 3 frogs appear. Then, he made 2 more appear. How many frogs were there altogether?

$$3 + 2 = 5 \text{ frogs}$$

1. Marta the Magnificent made 9 gorillas appear. Then, she made 3 of them disappear. How many gorillas were left?

_____

2. The Amazing Aaron made 5 snakes appear. Then, he made 5 more appear. How many snakes were there altogether?

_____

3. Tia the Terrific made 10 lions appear. Then, she made 2 of them disappear. How many lions were left?

_____

4. Awesome Amy made 8 lizards appear. Then, she made 7 of them disappear. How many lizards were left?

_____

5. Garrett the Great made 4 spiders appear. Then, he made 6 more appear. How many spiders were there altogether?

_____

Name _____   Date _____

More Magic Show Math

Directions:

Draw a picture to solve each problem. Write a number sentence to show the answer.

1. Warren the Wiz turned 4 friends into rabbits. Then, he turned 3 more friends into rabbits. How many friends were turned into rabbits?

_____

2. Darren the Daring turned 10 friends into eagles. Then, he changed 4 of them back. How many friends were still eagles?

_____

3. Super Susan turned 3 friends into butterflies. Then, she turned 6 more friends into butterflies. How many friends were turned into butterflies?

_____

4. Talented Tanya turned 9 friends into pigs. Then, she changed 6 of them back. How many friends were still pigs?

_____

5. Tricky Thomas turned 10 friends into tigers. Then, she changed 5 of them back. How many friends were still tigers?

_____

6. Ian the Incredible turned 2 friends into horses. Then, he turned 6 more into horses. How many friends were turned into horses?

_____

Writing and Solving Math Stories

Solving Number Sentences

Directions:
Solve each number sentence. Then, write a math story about your favorite topic to go with it.

Example:
7 + 2 = <u>9</u>   I had 7 computer games. My friend gave me 2 more. Now, I have 9 computer games.

1. 6 + 6 = _____ _____

_____

_____

2. 12 – 7 = _____ _____

_____

_____

3. 9 – 3 = _____ _____

_____

_____

4. 8 + 3 = _____ _____

_____

_____

Tackle the Solution

Directions:
Draw a picture to help solve each problem. Write the answer in the blank.

Example: $4 + \underline{2} = 6$

○○   ○
○○   ○

1. $5 = 2 + \underline{\hspace{1.2cm}}$

2. $3 + \underline{\hspace{1.2cm}} = 9$

3. $8 = 6 + \underline{\hspace{1.2cm}}$

4. $\underline{\hspace{1.2cm}} + 4 = 4$

5. $7 = \underline{\hspace{1.2cm}} + 1$

6. $\underline{\hspace{1.2cm}} + 2 = 10$

7. $8 = \underline{\hspace{1.2cm}} + 4$

8. $6 + 3 = \underline{\hspace{1.2cm}}$

9. $\underline{\hspace{1.2cm}} = 5 + 5$

Swish the Solution

Directions:
Draw a picture to help solve each problem. Write the answer in the blank.

Example: $9 - 6 =$ ___3___

⊗ ⊗ ⊗
⊗ ⊗ ⊗
○ ○ ○

1. _____ $= 6 - 2$

2. $7 - 4 =$ _____

3. _____ $= 9 - 7$

4. $5 -$ _____ $= 2$

5. $1 = 4 -$ _____

6. $6 -$ _____ $= 6$

7. $7 = 8 -$ _____

8. _____ $- 3 = 3$

9. $1 =$ _____ $- 4$

Name _____   Date _____

Take a Swing at the Solution

Directions:
Draw a picture to help solve each problem.
Write the answer in the blank.

1. $3 + \underline{\hspace{1.5cm}} = 4$

2. $6 = 2 + \underline{\hspace{1.5cm}}$

3. $7 - \underline{\hspace{1.5cm}} = 5$

4. $7 = \underline{\hspace{1.5cm}} + 3$

5. $8 - \underline{\hspace{1.5cm}} = 3$

6. $5 = 1 + \underline{\hspace{1.5cm}}$

7. $6 - 1 = \underline{\hspace{1.5cm}}$

8. $4 = \underline{\hspace{1.5cm}} - 4$

9. $\underline{\hspace{1.5cm}} + 2 = 9$

10. $\underline{\hspace{1.5cm}} = 8 - 7$

Fishing for Solutions

Directions:
Pick the fish with the correct solution and shade it. Write the solution in the blank to complete each number sentence.

1. $7 + 5 =$ _____

2. _____ $= 6 - 5$

3. $3 +$ _____ $= 8$

4. $6 = 4 +$ _____

5. _____ $+ 1 = 9$

6. $5 =$ _____ $+ 2$

7. _____ $- 2 = 9$

8. $6 =$ _____ $- 6$

Amazing Zero!

Directions:
Solve each problem with the greatest of ease by using zero as your helper!

1. $7 +$ _____ $= 7$

2. $6 - 6 =$ _____

3. $18 +$ _____ $= 18$

4. $20 - 20 =$ _____

5. $9 + 0 =$ _____

6. $12 - 0 =$ _____

7. _____ $+ 0 = 10$

8. $5 -$ _____ $= 0$

9. $13 + 0 =$ _____

10. $9 - 0 =$ _____

11. _____ $+ 23 = 23$

12. $11 -$ _____ $= 0$

13. $15 +$ _____ $= 15$

14. $8 -$ _____ $= 8$

15. $6 + 0 =$ _____

16. $14 -$ _____ $= 0$

17. _____ $+ 3 = 3$

18. _____ $- 0 = 4$

19. _____ $+ 0 = 12$

20. _____ $- 3 = 0$

The Return of Zero

Directions:
Solve each problem with the greatest of ease by using zero as your helper!

1. _____ $= 8 + 0$

2. _____ $= 2 - 2$

3. _____ $= 0 + 12$

4. _____ $= 12 - 0$

5. $6 = 6 +$ _____

6. $8 = 8 -$ _____

7. $9 = 0 +$ _____

8. $14 = 14 -$ _____

9. $7 =$ _____ $+ 0$

10. $3 =$ _____ $- 0$

11. $3 =$ _____ $+ 3$

12. $0 =$ _____ $- 5$

13. $13 = 13 +$ _____

14. $9 = 9 -$ _____

15. $10 = 0 +$ _____

16. $15 = 15 -$ _____

17. $4 =$ _____ $+ 0$

18. $6 =$ _____ $- 0$

19. $11 =$ _____ $+ 11$

20. $0 =$ _____ $- 4$

Name _____   Date _____

Directions:
Silly and Dilly counted some things they own and made graphs to compare their totals. Look at the graphs and answer the questions about them.

1.   Games

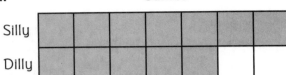

Who has more? _____

How many more? _____

Who has less? _____

How many less? _____

2.   Hats

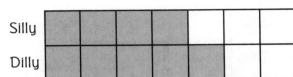

Who has more? _____

How many more? _____

Who has less? _____

How many less? _____

3.   Balls

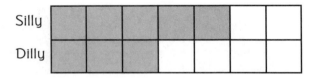

Who has more? _____

How many more? _____

Who has less? _____

How many less? _____

4.   Videos

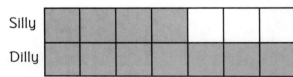

Who has more? _____

How many more? _____

Who has less? _____

How many less? _____

5.   Hamsters

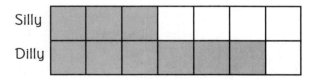

Who has more? _____

How many more? _____

Who has less? _____

How many less? _____

6.   Posters

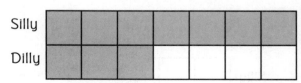

Who has more? _____

How many more? _____

Who has less? _____

How many less? _____

More of Silly and Dilly

Differences

Directions:

Silly and Dilly counted more of their things. Read the clues. Then, shade in the squares to help Silly and Dilly complete their graphs.

1.   **T-Shirts**

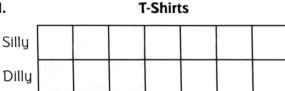

Silly has 5.
Dilly has 2 more.

2.   **Toy Cars**

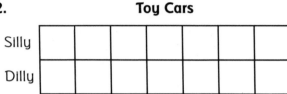

Dilly has 6.
Silly has 1 more.

3.   **Building Sets**

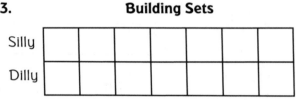

Silly has 4.
Dilly has 3 more.

4.   **Books**

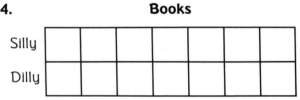

Dilly has 3.
Silly has 3 more.

5.   **Stuffed Animals**

Silly has 7.
Dilly has 2 less.

6.   **Puzzles**

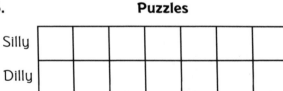

Dilly has 6.
Silly has 2 less.

7.   **CDs**

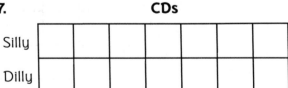

Silly has 7.
Dilly has 3 less.

8.   **Sweatshirts**

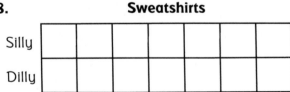

Dilly has 5.
Silly has 1 less.

Name _____   Date _____

Directions:
Sue and Lou counted the stickers in their collections. Read the clues. Then, shade in the squares on the graphs to help answer the questions.

1. **Fish Stickers**

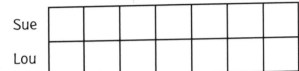

Sue
Lou

Sue has 3.
Lou has 2 more.
How many does Lou have? _____

2. **Dog Stickers**

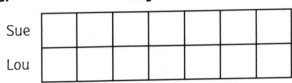

Sue
Lou

Sue has 6.
Lou has 2 less.
How many does Lou have? _____

3. **Dinosaur Stickers**

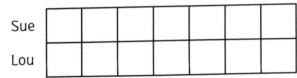

Sue
Lou

Sue has 4.
Lou has 3 more.
How many does Lou have? _____

4. **Space Stickers**

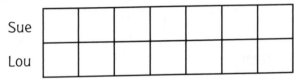

Sue
Lou

Sue has 6.
Lou has 3 less.
How many does Lou have? _____

5. **Cat Stickers**

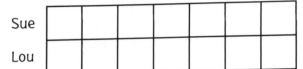

Sue
Lou

Lou has 6.
Sue has 1 more.
How many does Sue have? _____

6. **Elephant Stickers**

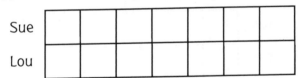

Sue
Lou

Lou has 7.
Sue has 2 less.
How many does Sue have? _____

7. **Ocean Stickers**

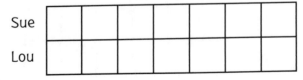

Sue
Lou

Lou has 4.
Sue has 3 less.
How many does Sue have? _____

8. **Bird Stickers**

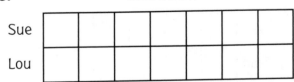

Sue
Lou

Lou has 5.
Sue has 1 more.
How many does Sue have? _____

Comparing Candy

Differences

Directions:

Juan and Tiara counted their candy. Read the clues. Then, shade in the squares on the graphs to help answer the questions.

1.   **Suckers**

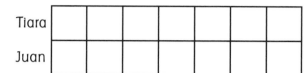

Tiara has 6.
That is 2 more than Juan has.
How many does Juan have? _____

2.   **Candy Bars**

Juan has 4.
That is 3 less than Tiara has.
How many does Tiara have? _____

3.   **Sticks of Gum**

Tiara has 2.
That is 5 less than Juan has.
How many does Juan have? _____

4.   **Peanut Butter Cups**

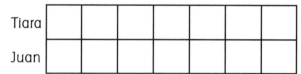

Juan has 7.
That is 3 more than Tiara has.
How many does Tiara have? _____

5.   **Chocolate Kisses**

Tiara has 7.
That is 1 more than Juan has.
How many does Juan have? _____

6.   **Hard Candies**

Juan has 1.
That is 5 less than Tiara has.
How many does Tiara have? _____

7.   **Taffy**

Tiara has 3.
That is 2 less than Juan has.
How many does Juan have? _____

8.   **Sour Balls**

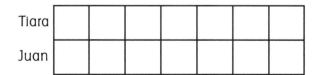

Juan has 6.
That is 4 more than Tiara has.
How many does Tiara have? _____

Party Stuff!

Directions:

The Party Stuff Store counted up all of their party stuff and made some graphs to compare the totals. Find the difference for each graph. Write an addition sentence and a subtraction sentence about each difference. Circle the difference in each sentence.

Example:

red balloons
yellow balloons

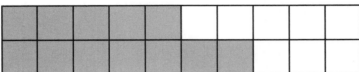

Difference is ___2___.

$5 + ②= 7$

$7 - ② = 5$

blue streamers
purple streamers

1. Difference is _____.

_____ + _____ = _____

_____ − _____ = _____

plastic goody bags
paper goody bags

2. Difference is _____.

_____ + _____ = _____

_____ − _____ = _____

paper confetti
foil confetti

3. Difference is _____.

_____ + _____ = _____

_____ − _____ = _____

tiaras
cone party hats

4. Difference is _____.

_____ + _____ = _____

_____ − _____ = _____

paper plates
plastic cups

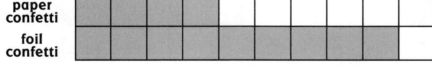

5. Difference is _____.

_____ + _____ = _____

_____ − _____ = _____

A Difference of 1

Differences

Directions:

Think of numbers that have a difference of 1. Write subtraction sentences with these numbers. Make each sentence different.

Examples:

3 and 2 have a difference of 1.   3 – 2 = 1
5 and 4 have a difference of 1.   5 – 4 = 1

1. _____ – _____ = 1   2. _____ – _____ = 1

3. _____ – _____ = 1   4. _____ – _____ = 1

5. _____ – _____ = 1   6. _____ – _____ = 1

7. _____ – _____ = 1   8. _____ – _____ = 1

9. _____ – _____ = 1   10. _____ – _____ = 1

11. _____ – _____ = 1   12. _____ – _____ = 1

13. _____ – _____ = 1   14. _____ – _____ = 1

15. _____ – _____ = 1   16. _____ – _____ = 1

A Difference of 2

Directions:
Think of numbers that have a difference of 2. Write subtraction sentences with these numbers. Make each sentence different.

Examples:
6 and 4 have a difference of 2.   6 – 4 = 2
10 and 8 have a difference of 2.   10 – 8 = 2

1. _____ – _____ = 2

2. _____ – _____ = 2

3. _____ – _____ = 2

4. _____ – _____ = 2

5. _____ – _____ = 2

6. _____ – _____ = 2

7. _____ – _____ = 2

8. _____ – _____ = 2

9. _____ – _____ = 2

10. _____ – _____ = 2

11. _____ – _____ = 2

12. _____ – _____ = 2

13. _____ – _____ = 2

14. _____ – _____ = 2

15. _____ – _____ = 2

16. _____ – _____ = 2

3, More or Less

Differences

Directions:

Look at each number in the middle column. Write the number that is 3 less and the number that is 3 more for each. The first one has been done for you.

	3 Less		3 More			3 Less		3 More
1.	1	4	7		2.	_____	3	_____
3.	_____	6	_____		4.	_____	7	_____
5.	_____	5	_____		6.	_____	10	_____
7.	_____	8	_____		8.	_____	13	_____
9.	_____	11	_____		10.	_____	22	_____
11.	_____	15	_____		12.	_____	35	_____
13.	_____	20	_____		14.	_____	40	_____
15.	_____	50	_____		16.	_____	56	_____
17.	_____	75	_____		18.	_____	68	_____
19.	_____	83	_____		20.	_____	97	_____

Design with a Difference of 4

Differences

Directions:
Find two numbers around the square that have a difference of 4. Connect their dots with a straight line. Write a subtraction sentence below to show they have a difference of 4. Repeat until each dot has been connected to another. Some dots may be connected to two dots. Color your design.

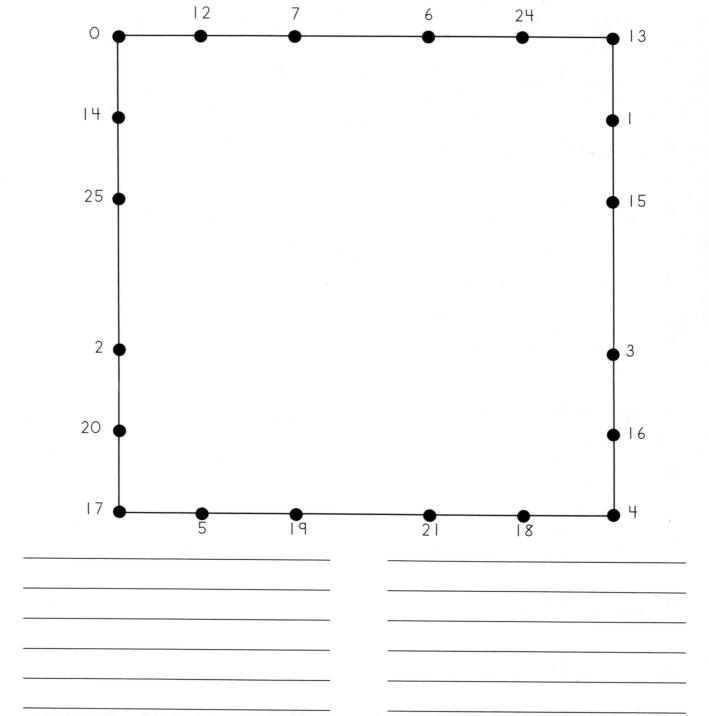

_____   _____

_____   _____

_____   _____

_____   _____

_____   _____

_____   _____

5, More or Less

Differences

Directions:
Look at each number in the middle column. Write the number that is 5 less and the number that is 5 more for each.

5 Less	5 More		5 Less	5 More
1. _____ 6 _____			2. _____ 8 _____	
3. _____ 7 _____			4. _____ 9 _____	
5. _____ 11 _____			6. _____ 15 _____	
7. _____ 12 _____			8. _____ 14 _____	
9. _____ 19 _____			10. _____ 22 _____	
11. _____ 25 _____			12. _____ 28 _____	
13. _____ 30 _____			14. _____ 36 _____	
15. _____ 41 _____			16. _____ 45 _____	
17. _____ 53 _____			18. _____ 67 _____	
19. _____ 88 _____			20. _____ 94 _____	

Difference Puzzles

Differences

Directions:
Shade the two numbers in each puzzle that have the correct difference.

Example:

3	4
8	5

Difference of 2

1.

9	6
5	11

Difference of 1

2.

7	11
2	4

Difference of 3

3.

10	2
7	3

Difference of 4

4.

5	4
6	6

Difference of 0

5.

1	2
5	7

Difference of 5

6.

8	7
3	5

Difference of 1

7.

6	2
10	3

Difference of 3

8.

10	4
5	3

Difference of 5

9.

8	5
6	2

Difference of 2

10.

6	9
5	11

Difference of 4

11.

4	10
7	3

Difference of 6

12.

7	8
10	8

Difference of 0

13.

6	10
0	3

Difference of 10

Name _____ Date _____

Tara's Pine Tree

Directions:
Tara and her dad planted a tiny pine tree in their yard on her sixth birthday. They measured it every year on her birthday to see how many inches it had grown. Look at the graph they made and answer the questions below.

Growth of Tara's Pine Tree

Number of Inches

	5	10	15	20	25	30

Birthday

Sixth

Seventh

Eighth

Ninth

Tenth

1. How tall was the tree when Tara planted it? _____

2. How tall was the tree on Tara's eighth birthday? _____

3. On which birthday was the tree 19 inches tall? _____

4. How many inches did the tree grow from Tara's sixth birthday to her seventh? _____

5. How many inches did the tree grow from Tara's sixth birthday to her eighth? _____

6. How many inches did the tree grow from Tara's seventh birthday to her ninth? _____

7. How many inches did the tree grow from Tara's ninth birthday to her tenth? _____

8. How many inches did the tree grow from Tara's sixth birthday to her tenth? _____

Andy the Baby Dinosaur

Investigating Change

Directions:

The chart below shows how Andy grew in length over six months. Use the chart to answer the questions.

Month	January	February	March	April	May	June
Length in Feet	1	2	5	11	21	35

1. How long was Andy in April? _____

2. In which month was Andy 21 feet long? _____

3. Which month was Andy longer: February or March? _____

4. Which month was Andy shorter: April or May? _____

5. How much did Andy grow from January to February? _____

6. How much did Andy grow from February to March? _____

7. How much did Andy grow from January to April? _____

8. How much did Andy grow from February to May? _____

9. From what month to what month did Andy grow 14 feet?

_____ to _____

10. From what month to what month did Andy grow 30 feet?

_____ to _____

Name _____ Date _____

Sandy the Baby Dinosaur

Directions:
The chart below shows how Sandy grew in weight over six months. Use the chart to answer the questions.

Month	January	February	March	April	May	June
Weight in Pounds	10	15	30	50	80	120

1. How much did Sandy weigh in March? _____

2. In which month did Sandy weigh 80 pounds? _____

3. Which month did Sandy weigh more: March or April? _____

4. Which month did Sandy weigh less: February or May? _____

5. How much weight did Sandy gain from January to February? _____

6. How much weight did Sandy gain from January to April? _____

7. How much weight did Sandy gain from January to June? _____

8. How much weight did Sandy gain from March to May? _____

9. From what month to what month did Sandy gain 20 pounds?

    _____ to _____

10. From what month to what month did Sandy gain 65 pounds?

    _____ to _____

Mandy the Baby Dinosaur

Investigating Change

Directions:
The chart below shows the number of teeth Mandy grew over six months. Use the chart to answer the questions.

Month	January	February	March	April	May	June
Number of Teeth	2	20	45	100	200	500

1. How many teeth did Mandy have in May? _____

2. In which month did Mandy have 45 teeth? _____

3. How many more teeth did Mandy have in February than in January? _____

4. How many more teeth did Mandy have in March than in February? _____

5. How many more teeth did Mandy have in April than in March? _____

6. How many more teeth did Mandy have in May than in April? _____

7. How many more teeth did Mandy have in June than in May? _____

8. How many more teeth did Mandy have in June than in January? _____

9. From what month to what month did Mandy's number of teeth double?

_____   to   _____

10. From what month to what month did Mandy's number of teeth grow 10 times?

_____   to   _____

Rosa's Snow Graph

Investigating Change

Directions:

Rosa made a graph of how much snow fell in her backyard one winter. Use the graph to answer the questions below.

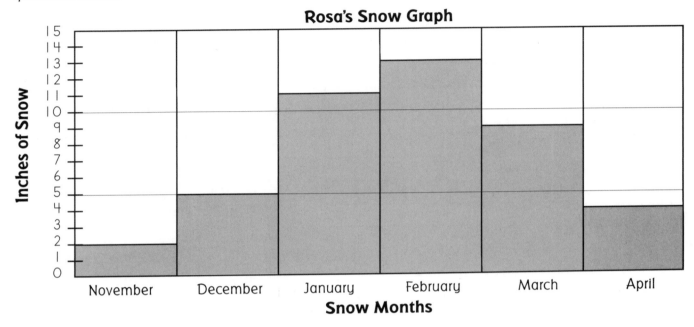

Rosa's Snow Graph

1. Which month had the most snow? _____

2. Which month had the least snow? _____

3. How much more snow was there in December than in November? _____

4. How much more snow was there in January than in December? _____

5. How much more snow was there in February than in January? _____

6. How much less snow was there in March than in February? _____

7. How much less snow was there in April than in March? _____

8. How many months had more than 10 inches of snow? _____

9. How many months had less than 5 inches of snow? _____

10. How much snow fell altogether? _____

Dion's Temperature Table

Directions:

Dion kept track of the temperatures in his town one week in the summer. Use the table he made to answer the questions below.

Day	High Temperature (°F)
Sunday	75
Monday	80
Tuesday	82
Wednesday	79
Thursday	85
Friday	91
Saturday	86

1. Did the temperature go up or down from Sunday to Monday? _____

2. Did the temperature go up or down from Tuesday to Wednesday? _____

3. Did the temperature go up or down from Thursday to Friday? _____

4. Did the temperature go up or down from Friday to Saturday? _____

5. How much did the temperature go up from Sunday to Monday? _____

6. How much did the temperature go up from Monday to Tuesday? _____

7. How much did the temperature go down from Tuesday to Wednesday? _____

8. How much did the temperature go down from Friday to Saturday? _____

9. On which days was the temperature above 83°? _____

_____

10. On which days was the temperature below 83°? _____

_____

Name _____   Date _____

Casey's Caps

Directions:

Casey sold caps for a week to raise money for a scouting trip. He made a table to show how many caps he sold each day. Use the table to answer the questions below.

Day	Number of Caps Sold
Sunday	4
Monday	8
Tuesday	3
Wednesday	6
Thursday	2
Friday	12
Saturday	13

1. Did Casey's sales go up or down from Sunday to Monday? _____

2. Did Casey's sales go up or down from Monday to Tuesday? _____

3. Did Casey's sales go up or down from Thursday to Friday? _____

4. Did Casey's sales go up or down from Friday to Saturday? _____

5. How many more caps did Casey sell on Sunday than on Tuesday? _____

6. How many more caps did Casey sell on Saturday than on Thursday? _____

7. How many fewer caps did Casey sell on Monday than on Friday? _____

8. How many fewer caps did Casey sell on Thursday than on Sunday? _____

9. On which two days put together did Casey sell 25 caps in all? _____

_____

10. On which three days put together did Casey sell less than 10 caps? _____

_____

Sticker Story

Directions:

I have some stickers. ☐ stands for my stickers.

You have some stickers. △ stands for your stickers.

$$\square + 5 = \triangle$$

This number sentence tells about my stickers and your stickers.

Use the number sentence above to help fill in this chart to tell how many stickers we both have.

☐	0	1	2	3	4	5						
△	5	6	7									

1. If I have 4 stickers, how many stickers do you have? _9 stickers_

2. If I have 8 stickers, how many stickers do you have? _20 stickers_

3. If you have 7 stickers, how many stickers do I have? _105 stickers_

4. If you have 11 stickers, how many stickers do I have? _____

5. If I have 100 stickers, how many stickers do you have? _____

6. If you have 25 stickers, how many stickers do I have? _____

7. How many more stickers will you always have than I? _____

8. How many fewer stickers will I always have than you? _____

9. Write a subtraction number sentence to go with the addition sentence in the directions.

_____

Football Cards

Directions:

I have some football cards. ☐ stands for my football cards.

You have some football cards. △ stands for your football cards.

$$\square - 3 = \triangle$$ This number sentence tells about my football cards and your football cards.

Use the number sentence above to help fill in this chart to tell how many football cards we both have.

☐	3	4	5	6	7	8						
△	0	1	2									

1. If I have 7 football cards, how many do you have? _____

2. If I have 11 football cards, how many do you have? _____

3. If you have 2 football cards, how many do I have? _____

4. If you have 9 football cards, how many do I have? _____

5. If I have 20 football cards, how many do you have? _____

6. If you have 100 football cards, how many do I have? _____

7. How many fewer football cards will you always have than me? _____

8. How many more football cards will I always have than you? _____

9. Write an addition number sentence to go with the subtraction sentence in the directions.

_____

Mystery Shapes and Numbers

Variables

Directions:

Look at the number sentences below. The same shapes stand for the same numbers. Use the number sentences to answer the questions.

$$3 + \square = 7 \quad \text{and} \quad \square + \triangle = 10$$

1. What number does $\square$ stand for? _____

2. What number does $\triangle$ stand for? _____

3. How much would $\square + \square$ be? _____

4. How much would $\triangle + \square$ be? _____

5. How much would $\triangle + \triangle$ be? _____

6. How much would $\triangle - \square$ be? _____

7. How much would $\square + \square + \square$ be? _____

8. How much would $\triangle + \square + \square$ be? _____

9. How much would $\triangle + \triangle + \square$ be? _____

10. How much would $\triangle + \triangle + \triangle$ be? _____

Mystery Shapes and Numbers 2

 Variables

Directions:
Look at the number sentences below. The same shapes stand for the same numbers. Use the number sentences to answer the questions.

$$9 - \square = 3 \quad \text{and} \quad \square + \triangle = 8$$

1. What number does $\square$ stand for? _____

2. What number does $\triangle$ stand for? _____

3. How much would $\square + \square$ be? _____

4. How much would $\triangle + \square$ be? _____

5. How much would $\triangle + \triangle$ be? _____

6. How much would $\square - \triangle$ be? _____

7. How much would $\square + \square + \square$ be? _____

8. How much would $\triangle + \square + \square$ be? _____

9. How much would $\triangle + \triangle + \square$ be? _____

10. How much would $\triangle + \triangle + \triangle$ be? _____

Mystery Shapes and Numbers 3

Variables

Directions:

Look at the number sentences below. The same shapes stand for the same numbers. Use the number sentences to answer the questions.

$$\square + \square = 8 \quad \text{and} \quad \square + \triangle + \triangle = 14$$

1. What number does $\square$ stand for? _____

2. How did you figure it out? _____

3. What number does $\triangle$ stand for? _____

4. How did you figure it out? _____

5. How much would $\square + \triangle$ be? _____

6. How much would $\triangle - \square$ be? _____

7. How much would $\triangle - \triangle$ be? _____

8. How much would $\square + \square + \square$ be? _____

9. How much would $\triangle + \triangle + \triangle$ be? _____

10. How much would $\square + \square + \triangle$ be? _____

11. Which would be more: $\square + \square + \square + \square$ or $\triangle + \triangle + \triangle + \triangle$? Why?

_____

_____

_____

Shape Stumpers

Variables

Directions:
Look at the number sentences below. The same shapes stand for the same numbers. Figure out what number each shape stands for and rewrite the number sentences using the correct numbers. Then, answer the questions.

$12 = \square + \square$ $12 = $ _____ + _____

$12 = \triangle + \triangle + \square$ $12 = $ _____ + _____ + _____

$12 = \bigcirc + \bigcirc + \bigcirc$ $12 = $ _____ + _____ + _____

1. How did you figure out $\square$? _____

_____

2. How did you figure out $\triangle$? _____

_____

3. How did you figure out $\bigcirc$? _____

_____

- -

$16 = \pentagon + \pentagon$ $16 = $ _____ + _____

$16 = \pentagon + \triangle + \triangle$ $16 = $ _____ + _____ + _____

$16 = \pentagon + \triangle + \octagon + \octagon$ $16 = $ _____ + _____ + _____ + _____

4. How did you figure out $\pentagon$? _____

_____

5. How did you figure out $\triangle$? _____

_____

6. How did you figure out $\octagon$? _____

_____

Note: When students are asked to write number sentences, any equation equivalent to the one listed is also correct.

Page 5
Shapes should be pasted in the correct sets. Six shapes should be outside of the sets because they are neither triangles nor squares.

Page 6
Letters should be pasted in the correct sets. Four boxes should be outside of the sets because they contain numbers instead of letters.

Page 7
Numbers should be pasted in the correct sets. One number should be outside of the sets because it is exactly 10—not less or greater than.

Page 8
A. Even—6, 8, 2, 4, 10, 24, 36
   Odd—5, 3, 7, 15, 37, 41, 1, 11, 25
B. Greater than 7—11, 12, 100, 50, 8, 10, 9, 15, 20
   Less than 7—6, 2, 1, 0, 5, 3, 4
C. Does not have exactly 2 ones—21, 5, 38, 3, 24, 19, 200
   Has exactly 2 ones—52, 42, 22, 12, 2, 62, 32, 72, 162

Page 9
1. all uppercase letters
2. all rectangles
3. numbers less than 10
4. all smiles

Page 10
1. even numbers
2. numbers greater than 50
3. 3 in the tens place
4. answers when counting by 5

Page 11
6, 4, 3, 8, 5
1. triangle
2. octagon
3. T, S, P, H, O
4. 2   5. 2
6. 2   7. 4
8. 3

Page 12
You, Zou, Bou, Sou
Ted, Ned, Zed, Red, Hed

Page 13
1. H
2. M
3. M, C, H
4. C > M, H > M, M < H, H > C
5. A, N, Z, Y
6. Z > Y, A > Y, N < A, N > Z, Z < N

Page 14
1. RYRYRYRY
2. BGRBGRBG
3. BBYBBYBB
4. RYYRYYRY
5. BBGGBBGG
6. Answers will vary.

Page 15
1. ABABABAB   2. DDCDDCD
3. FEEFEE   4. GHHHGH
5. IIJJII   6. KLMKLMKL
7. NNOPNN   8. RSTQR

Page 16
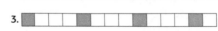
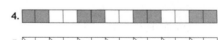

Page 17
1. C; Answers will vary.
2. E; Answers will vary.
3. G; Answers will vary.
4. I; Answers will vary.

Pages 18-20
Answers will vary.

Page 21
1. 0, 2, 4, 6, 8
2. 12, 14, 18, 20, 24, 26, 28; 34, 36, 40, 42, 44, 48, 50; 62, 64, 66, 70, 72, 76, 78
3. 36, 18, 30, 44, 10, 50, 56, 64, 78
4. 12, 24, 30, 4, 18, 38, 50, 58, 86
5. Answers will vary.

Page 22
1. 1, 3, 5, 7, 9
2. 13, 15, 19, 21, 25, 27, 29; 37, 39, 43, 45, 49, 51, 53; 77, 79, 83, 85, 87, 91, 93
3. 9, 15, 27, 33, 49, 51, 55, 63, 77
4. 3, 15, 21, 29, 43, 47, 55, 81, 93
5. Answers will vary.

Page 23
1. 12 corners
2. 24 corners
3. 30 corners
4. 33 corners
5. 2 triangles
6. 5 triangles
7. 10 triangles
8. 12 triangles
9. 150 corners
10. 100 triangles

Page 24
1. 16 corners
2. 28 corners
3. 40 corners
4. 48 corners
5. 3 squares
6. 6 squares
7. 10 squares
8. 13 squares
9. 120 corners
10. 25 squares

Page 25
1. 25 corners
2. 40 corners
3. 50 corners
4. 65 corners
5. 4 pentagons
6. 7 pentagons
7. 10 pentagons
8. 14 pentagons
9. 100 corners
10. 30 pentagons

Page 26
1. 24 corners
2. 54 corners
3. 60 corners
4. 66 corners
5. 5 hexagons
6. 8 hexagons
7. 10 hexagons
8. 12 hexagons
9. 120 corners
10. 100 hexagons

Page 27
1. 45¢
2. 55¢
3. 60¢
4. 40¢
5. 60¢
6. 70¢
7. Diane
8. Dion
9. Diamond and Nita

Page 28
1. 10, 12, 14, 16, 18, 20, 22, 24, 26, 28
2. 9, 11, 13, 15, 17, 19, 21, 23, 25, 27
3. 15, 18, 21, 24, 30, 33, 36, 39, 42
4. 25, 30, 35, 40, 45, 50, 55, 60, 65, 70
5. 50, 60, 70, 80, 90, 100, 110, 120, 130, 140
6. 20, 24, 28, 32, 36, 40, 44, 48, 52, 56
7. 30, 36, 42, 48, 54, 60, 66, 72, 78, 84
8. 58, 60, 62, 64, 66, 68, 70, 72, 74, 76
9. 69, 71, 73, 75, 77, 79, 81, 83, 85, 87

Page 29
1. Rainbows should be drawn; 0 + 5, 1 + 4, 2 + 3
2. Rainbows should be drawn; 0 + 6, 1 + 5, 2 + 4, 3 + 3
3. Rainbows should be drawn; 0 + 7, 1 + 6, 2 + 5, 3 + 4

Page 30
1. Rainbows should be drawn; 0 + 8, 1 + 7, 2 + 6, 3 + 5, 4 + 4
2. Rainbows should be drawn; 0 + 9, 1 + 8, 2 + 7, 3 + 6, 4 + 5
3. Rainbows should be drawn; 0 + 10, 1 + 9, 2 + 8, 3 + 7, 4 + 6, 5 + 5

Page 31
1. 8
2. 5
3. 13
4. 5
5. 17
6. 0
7. 8, 16, 21, 40, 53
8. 5, 9, 13, 24, 29
9. 14, 30, 44, 62, 80

Page 32
1. 4
2. 10
3. 8
4. 10
5. 3
6. 13
7. 1, 2, 3, 4, 5
8. 0, 1, 2, 3, 4
9. 17, 18, 19, 20, 21

Page 33
1. +1
2. +3
3. +10
4. −6
5. −5
6. −8
7. +1; 30, 57, 39
8. +10; 72, 89, 40
9. −4; 11, 16, 35

Page 34
Gummy Snakes: 9¢, 12¢, 15¢, 18¢
Gummy Beetles: 12¢, 16¢, 20¢, 24¢
1. 9¢, 16¢, 15¢, 24¢, 21¢, 32¢, 30¢, 40¢
2. 3 gummy beetles, 4 gummy beetles, neither, 6 gummy snakes
3. 21¢, 23¢

Page 35
Gummy Frogs: 10¢, 15¢, 20¢, 25¢, 30¢
Gummy Turtles: 20¢, 30¢, 40¢, 50¢, 60¢
1. 4, 2
2. 6, 3
3. 35¢, 70¢, 50¢, $1.00
4. 3 gummy frogs, neither
5. 40¢, 75¢

Page 36
1. 0–6 should be circled; 7 should have a triangle around it; 8–14 should have boxes around them.
2. 19–24 should be circled; 25 should have a triangle around it; 26–31 should have boxes around them.
3. 27–29 should be circled; 30 should have a triangle around it; 31–39 should have boxes around them.
4. 38–45 should be circled; 46 should have a triangle around it; 47–50 should have boxes around them.

Page 37
1. M < A
2. B > R
3. C < H
4. C = P
5. E > R

Page 38
1. X < W
2. V = U
3. T < S
4. R = Q
5. P > O
6. N < M
7. L = K
8. J > 1
9. H < G
10. F > E
11. D = C

Page 39
1. B < T, B > L, L < T
2. S < R, S = C, R > C
3. N > L, 1 > L, L < A

Page 40
1. 6
2. 14
3. 5
4. 14
5. 27
6. 32

Page 41
1. 4 square crackers
2. 1 square cracker
3. 3 circle crackers
4. 4 crackers
5. yes
6. 3 + 1
7. 4 = 4, 4 = 3 + 1, 4 = 1 + 3

Page 42
1. 3 square crackers
2. 2 circle crackers
3. 5 crackers
4. 5 circle crackers
5. yes
6. 3 + 2
7. 5 = 5, 3 + 2 = 5, 2 + 3 = 5

Page 43
1. 6 circle cookies
2. 2 circle cookies
3. 3 triangle cookies
4. 1 square cookie
5. 6 cookies
6. yes
7. 2 + 1 + 3
8. 6 = 6, 6 = 2 + 3 + 1, 6 = 3 + 1 + 2

Page 44
1. 2 circle cookies
2. 2 triangle cookies
3. 3 square cookies
4. 7 cookies
5. 7 square cookies
6. yes
7. 2 + 2 + 3
8. 7 = 7, 2 + 2 + 3 = 7, 2 + 3 + 2 = 7

Page 45

1. 3 apples
2. 1 banana
3. 4 pieces of fruit
4. 3 + 1
5. 2 apples
6. 2 bananas
7. 4 pieces of fruit
8. 2 + 2
9. yes
10. 4 = 4, 4 = 2 + 2, 3 + 1 = 4, 3 + 1 = 2 + 2

Page 46

1. me: 4 of same shape; you: 3 of one shape and 1 of another shape
2. me: 2 of same shape; you: 1 of one shape and 1 of another shape
3. me: 4 of same shape; you: 2 of one shape and 2 of another shape
4. me: 5 of same shape; you: 4 of one shape and 1 of another shape
5. me: 5 of same shape; you: 3 of one shape and 2 of another shape
6. me: 6 of same shape; you: 5 of one shape and 1 of another shape
7. me: 6 of same shape; you: 4 of one shape and 2 of another shape

Page 47

1. 1 + 1 = 2; 2 = 2
2. 2 + 2 = 4; 4 = 4
3. 4 = 4; 1 + 3 = 4
4. 5 = 5; 3 + 2 = 5
5. 3 + 3 = 6; 6 = 6
6. 4 + 3 = 7; 7 = 7
7. 8 = 8, 5 + 3 = 8

Page 48

1. 3 + 2 = 4 + 1
2. 3 + 3 = 2 + 4
3. 5 + 2 = 4 + 3
4. 5 + 3 = 6 + 2
5. 4 + 4 = 7 + 1
6. 7 + 2 = 6 + 3
7. 8 + 1 = 5 + 4

Page 49

1. 4 oranges
2. 3 oranges
3. no
4. yes
5. 4 > 3
6. 1 orange
7. yes
8. 4 = 3 + 1

Page 50

1. 5 blocks
2. 3 blocks
3. no
4. yes
5. 5 > 3
6. 2 blocks
7. yes
8. 5 − 2 = 3

Page 51

1. 3 brownies
2. 6 brownies
3. no
4. yes
5. 3 < 6
6. 3 brownies
7. yes
8. 3 + 3 = 6

Page 52

1. 4 peanuts
2. 5 peanuts
3. no
4. yes
5. 4 < 5
6. 1 peanut
7. yes
8. 4 = 5 − 1

Page 53

1. 4 = 2 + 2
2. 4 = 6 − 2
3. 5 − 3 = 2
4. 1 + 5 = 6
5. 7 = 3 + 4
6. 3 = 7 − 4
7. 6 − 1 = 5

Page 54

1. yes
2. yes
3. no
4. yes
5. no
6. no
7. no
8. yes
9. no
10. no
11. no
12. yes

Page 55

1. no	2. yes
3. yes	4. no
5. yes	6. yes
7. no	8. no
9. yes	10. no
11. no	12. yes

Page 56

1. $3 + 2 = 4 + 1$	2. $6 + 5 = 5 + 6$
3. $7 + 0 = 3 + 4$	4. $4 + 4 = 7 + 1$
5. $2 + 7 = 7 + 2$	6. $6 + 3 = 5 + 4$

Page 57

1. $5 - 2 = 4 - 1$	2. $6 - 2 = 4 - 0$
3. $5 - 3 = 7 - 5$	4. $9 - 8 = 4 - 3$
5. $5 - 0 = 7 - 2$	6. $6 - 6 = 9 - 9$

Page 58

1. $2 + 2 = 7 - 3$	2. $8 - 5 = 2 + 1$
3. $1 + 1 = 7 - 5$	4. $5 + 3 = 4 + 4$
5. $2 - 0 = 8 - 6$	6. $2 + 3 = 9 - 4$

Page 59

$7 + 0 = 4 + 3$; $5 + 1 = 3 + 3$; $3 + 6 = 5 + 4$;
$4 + 4 = 6 + 2$; $2 + 3 = 3 + 2$; $3 + 1 = 2 + 2$

Page 60

$7 - 2 = 6 - 1$; $6 - 2 = 4 - 0$; $7 - 4 = 6 - 3$;
$4 - 2 = 3 - 1$; $7 - 1 = 10 - 4$; $3 - 2 = 5 - 4$

Page 61

$6 + 1 = 9 - 2$; $4 + 4 = 10 - 2$; $7 - 2 = 3 + 2$;
$2 + 2 = 5 - 1$; $6 - 3 = 2 + 1$; $7 - 1 = 3 + 3$

Pages 62-63

$4 = 2 + 2 = 5 - 1 = 3 + 1$
$5 = 7 - 2 = 2 + 3 = 1 + 4$
$6 = 7 - 1 = 3 + 3 = 6 + 0$
$7 = 5 + 2 = 4 + 3 = 9 - 2$
$8 = 4 + 4 = 9 - 1 = 2 + 6$
$9 = 5 + 4 = 10 - 1 = 3 + 6$

Page 64

$3 + 2 = 4 + 1$; $3 + 3 = 2 + 4$; $4 + 3 = 7 + 0$;
$5 + 4 = 3 + 6$; $6 + 2 = 4 + 4$

Page 65

$3 - 1 = 5 - 3$; $9 - 1 = 10 - 2$; $5 - 1 = 7 - 3$;
$10 - 3 = 8 - 1$; $3 - 0 = 6 - 3$; $10 - 1 = 12 - 3$;
$7 - 1 = 6 - 0$; $7 - 2 = 10 - 5$

Page 66

$8 - 1 = 3 + 4$; $4 + 4 = 10 - 2$; $4 + 1 = 6 - 1$;
$6 - 2 = 2 + 2$; $8 - 2 = 3 + 3$; $6 + 3 = 10 - 1$;
$3 - 0 = 2 + 1$; $12 - 2 = 5 + 5$

Page 67

$5 + 2 = 8 - 1$; $6 + 6 = 13 - 1$; $11 - 1 = 5 + 5$;
$8 - 2 = 3 + 3$; $9 + 2 = 14 - 3$; $6 + 3 = 11 - 2$;
$10 - 2 = 4 + 4$; $2 + 3 = 6 - 1$

Page 68

The following should be circled: $7 = 7$; $8 > 7$, $4 + 3 = 7$,
$7 = 4 + 3$; $7 = 3 + 4$; $4 + 3 = 4 + 3$; $4 + 3 = 3 + 4$
1. Because $7 = 7$
2. Because $7 \neq 8$

Page 69

The following should be circled: $9 = 9$; $9 > 8$;
$8 + 1 = 9$; $9 - 8 = 1$; $9 = 8 + 1$; $8 = 9 - 1$; $9 = 1 + 8$;
$8 + 1 = 10 - 1$
1. Because $9 = 9$
2. Because $1 \neq -1$ (or, you cannot subtract 9 from 8)
3. Because $10 \neq 7$

Pages 70-72

Answers will vary.

Page 73

1.–9. $8 + 0$; $0 + 8$; $1 + 7$; $7 + 1$; $2 + 6$; $6 + 2$; $5 + 3$;
$3 + 5$; $4 + 4$
10.–16. Answers will vary.

Page 74

1.–10. $0 + 9$; $9 + 0$; $1 + 8$; $8 + 1$; $7 + 2$; $2 + 7$; $3 + 6$;
$6 + 3$; $5 + 4$; $4 + 5$
11.–17. Answers will vary.

Page 75

1.–11. $0 + 10$; $10 + 0$; $9 + 1$; $1 + 9$; $8 + 2$; $2 + 8$; $3 + 7$;
$7 + 3$; $6 + 4$; $4 + 6$; $5 + 5$
12.–18. Answers will vary.

Page 76

1.–12. 11 + 0; 0 + 11; 1 + 10; 10 + 1; 9 + 2; 2 + 9; 3 + 8; 8 + 3; 4 + 7; 7 + 4; 6 + 5; 5 + 6

13.–19. Answers will vary.

Page 77

1.–13. 12 + 0; 0 + 12; 1 + 11; 11 + 1; 10 + 2; 2 + 10; 9 + 3; 3 + 9; 4 + 8; 8 + 4; 5 + 7; 7 + 5; 6 + 6

14.–20. Answers will vary.

Page 78

1. Picture should show 4 balloons and 3 balloons.
   4 + 3 = 7 balloons
2. Picture should show 2 balloons and 4 balloons.
   2 + 4 = 6 balloons
3. Picture should show 1 balloon and 7 balloons.
   1 + 7 = 8 balloons

Page 79

1. Picture should show 5 books with 1 crossed out.
   5 - 1 = 4 books
2. Picture should show 7 books with 4 crossed out.
   7 - 4 = 3 books
3. Picture should show 8 books with 3 crossed out.
   8 - 3 = 5 books

Page 80

1. Picture should show 3 balls and 5 balls.
   3 + 5 = 8 table tennis balls
2. Picture should show 7 balls with 2 crossed out.
   7 - 2 = 5 tennis balls
3. Picture should show 6 balls with 3 crossed out.
   6 - 3 = 3 baseballs
4. Picture should show 5 balls and 2 balls.
   5 + 2 = 7 footballs
5. Picture should show 8 balls with 2 crossed out.
   8 - 2 = 6 rubber balls
6. Picture should show 2 balls and 2 balls.
   2 + 2 = 4 kick balls

Page 81

Answers will vary.

Page 82

1. Picture should show 2 aunts and 4 uncles.
   6 aunts and uncles
2. Picture should show 2 grandmas and 2 grandpas.
   4 grandparents

Page 82 (cont.)

3. Picture should show 3 boy cousins and 4 girl cousins.
   7 cousins
4. Picture should show 6 neighbors and 3 neighbors.
   9 neighbors
5. Picture should show 1 brother and 6 sisters.
   7 brothers and sisters

Page 83

1. Picture should show 5 flies with 1 crossed out.
   4 flies
2. Picture should show 7 ants with 2 crossed out.
   5 ants
3. Picture should show 8 butterflies with 4 crossed out.
   4 butterflies
4. Picture should show 9 bees with 2 crossed out.
   7 bees
5. Picture should show 7 caterpillars with 4 crossed out.
   3 caterpillars

Page 84

1. Picture should show 6 T-shirts and 2 T-shirts.
   8 T-shirts
2. Picture should show 8 baseball caps with 3 crossed out.   5 clean baseball caps
3. Picture should show 6 soccer shirts with 3 crossed out.
   3 soccer shirts
4. Picture should show 3 pairs of shorts and 2 pairs of shorts.   5 pairs of shorts
5. Picture should show 5 sweatshirts and 4 sweatshirts.   9 sweatshirts
6. Picture should show 10 T-shirts with 4 crossed out.
   6 T-shirts

Page 85

1. Picture should show 9 gorillas with 3 crossed out.
   9 - 3 = 6 gorillas
2. Picture should show 5 snakes and 5 snakes.
   5 + 5 = 10 snakes
3. Picture should show 10 lions with 2 crossed out.
   10 - 2 = 8 lions
4. Picture should show 8 lizards with 7 crossed out.
   8 - 7 = 1 lizard
5. Picture should show 4 spiders and 6 spiders.
   4 + 6 = 10 spiders

Page 86
1. Picture should show 4 rabbits and 3 rabbits.
   4 + 3 = 7 friends
2. Picture should show 10 eagles with 4 crossed out.
   10 – 4 = 6 friends
3. Picture should show 3 butterflies and 6 butterflies.
   3 + 6 = 9 friends
4. Picture should show 9 pigs with 6 crossed out.
   9 – 6 = 3 friends
5. Picture should show 10 tigers with 5 crossed out.
   10 – 5 = 5 friends
6. Picture should show 2 horses and 6 horses.
   2 + 6 = 8 friends

Page 87
Answers will vary.

Page 88
1. 3	2. 6
3. 2	4. 0
5. 6	6. 8
7. 4	8. 9
9. 10	

Page 89
1. 4	2. 3
3. 2	4. 3
5. 3	6. 0
7. 1	8. 6
9. 5	

Page 90
1. 1	2. 4
3. 2	4. 4
5. 5	6. 4
7. 5	8. 8
9. 7	10. 1

Page 91
1. 4; yes	2. 1; yes
3. 5; yes	4. 1; no
5. 5; yes	6. 2; no
7. 6; no	8. 6; yes

Page 92
The following should be circled:
1. Minusman says 5.	2. Pluswoman says 5.
3. Pluswoman says 7.	4. Minusman says 6.
5. Minusman says 8.	6. Pluswoman says 8.
7. Minusman says 8.	8. Minusman says 7.

Minusman should be circled. Students should write 3 beside Pluswoman and 5 beside Minusman.

Page 93
1. 12	2. 1
3. 5	4. 2
5. 8	6. 3
7. 11	8. 12

Page 94
1. 0	2. 0
3. 0	4. 0
5. 9	6. 12
7. 10	8. 5
9. 13	10. 9
11. 0	12. 11
13. 0	14. 0
15. 6	16. 14
17. 0	18. 4
19. 12	20. 3

Page 95
1. 8	2. 0
3. 12	4. 12
5. 0	6. 0
7. 9	8. 0
9. 7	10. 3
11. 0	12. 5
13. 0	14. 0
15. 10	16. 0
17. 4	18. 6
19. 0	20. 4

Page 96
1. Silly; 2; Dilly; 2	2. Dilly; 1; Silly; 1
3. Silly; 2; Dilly; 2	4. Dilly; 3; Silly; 3
5. Dilly; 3; Silly; 3	6. Silly; 4; Dilly; 4

Page 97

1. T-Shirts
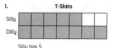
Silly has 5.
Dilly has 2 more.

2. Toy Cars
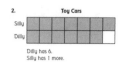
Dilly has 6.
Silly has 1 more.

3. Building Sets

Silly has 4.
Dilly has 3 more.

4. Books

Dilly has 3.
Silly has 3 more.

5. Stuffed Animals

Silly has 7.
Dilly has 2 less.

6. Puzzles
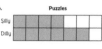
Dilly has 6.
Silly has 2 less.

7. CDs
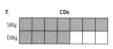
Silly has 7.
Dilly has 3 less.

8. Sweatshirts
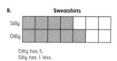
Dilly has 5.
Silly has 1 less.

Page 98

1. Fish Stickers

Sue has 3.
Lou has 2 more.
How many does Lou have? **5**

2. Dog Stickers
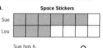
Sue has 6.
Lou has 2 less.
How many does Lou have? **4**

3. Dinosaur Stickers

Sue has 4.
Lou has 3 more.
How many does Lou have? **7**

4. Space Stickers

Sue has 6.
Lou has 3 less.
How many does Lou have? **3**

5. Cat Stickers
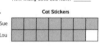
Lou has 6.
Sue has 1 more.
How many does Sue have? **7**

6. Elephant Stickers

Lou has 7.
Sue has 2 less.
How many does Sue have? **5**

7. Ocean Stickers

Lou has 4.
Sue has 3 less.
How many does Sue have? **1**

8. Bird Stickers
Lou has 5.
Sue has 1 more.
How many does Sue have? **6**

Page 99

1. Suckers

Tiara has 6.
That is 2 more than Juan has.
How many does Juan have? **4**

2. Candy Bars
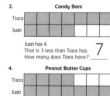
Juan has 4.
That is 3 less than Tiara has.
How many does Tiara have? **7**

3. Sticks of Gum

Tiara has 2.
That is 5 less than Juan has.
How many does Juan have? **7**

4. Peanut Butter Cups
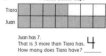
Juan has 7.
That is 3 more than Tiara has.
How many does Tiara have? **4**

5. Chocolate Kisses
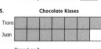
Tiara has 7.
That is 1 more than Juan has.
How many does Juan have? **6**

6. Hard Candies
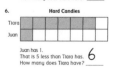
Juan has 1.
That is 5 less than Tiara has.
How many does Tiara have? **6**

7. Taffy

Tiara has 3.
That is 2 less than Juan has.
How many does Juan have? **5**

8. Sour Balls

Juan has 6.
That is 4 more than Tiara has.
How many does Tiara have? **2**

Page 100
1. 3; 2 + 3 = 5; 5 − 3 = 2
2. 1; 6 + 1 = 7; 7 − 1 = 6
3. 5; 4 + 5 = 9; 9 − 5 = 4
4. 4; 4 + 4 = 8; 8 − 4 = 4
5. 2; 6 + 2 = 8; 8 − 2 = 6

Pages 101 – 102
Answers will vary.

Page 103
1. 1; 7	2. 0; 6
3. 3; 9	4. 4; 10
5. 2; 8	6. 7; 13
7. 5; 11	8. 10; 16
9. 8; 14	10. 19; 25
11. 12; 18	12. 32; 38
13. 17; 23	14. 37; 43
15. 47; 53	16. 53; 59
17. 72; 78	18. 65; 71
19. 80; 86	20. 94; 100

Page 104
24 − 20 = 4; 4 − 0 = 4; 17 − 13 = 4; 5 − 1 = 4;
19 − 15 = 4; 7 − 3 = 4; 16 − 12 = 4; 25 − 21 = 4;
6 − 2 = 4; 18 − 14 = 4; 20 − 16 = 4; 21 − 17 = 4

Page 105
1. 1; 11	2. 3; 13
3. 2; 12	4. 4; 14
5. 6; 16	6. 10; 20
7. 7; 17	8. 9; 19
9. 14; 24	10. 17; 27
11. 20; 30	12. 23; 33
13. 25; 35	14. 31; 41
15. 36; 46	16. 40; 50
17. 48; 58	18. 62; 72
19. 83; 93	20. 89; 99

Page 106
1. 5; 6	2. 7; 4	13. 0; 10
3. 7; 3	4. 6; 6	
5. 2; 7	6. 8; 7	
7. 6; 3	8. 10; 5	
9. 8; 6	10. 9; 5	
11. 4; 10	12. 8; 8	

Page 107
1. 3 inches
2. 12 inches
3. ninth
4. 3 inches
5. 9 inches
6. 13 inches
7. 9 inches
8. 25 inches

Page 108
1. 11 feet
2. May
3. March
4. April
5. 1 foot
6. 3 feet
7. 10 feet
8. 19 feet
9. May to June
10. March to June

Page 109
1. 30 pounds
2. May
3. April
4. February
5. 5 pounds
6. 40 pounds
7. 110 pounds
8. 50 pounds
9. January to March or March to April
10. February to May

Page 110
1. 200 teeth
2. March
3. 8 teeth
4. 25 teeth
5. 55 teeth
6. 100 teeth
7. 300 teeth
8. 498 teeth
9. April to May
10. February to May or January to February

Page 111
1. February
2. November
3. 3 inches
4. 6 inches
5. 2 inches
6. 4 inches
7. 5 inches
8. 2 months
9. 2 months
10. 44 inches

Page 112
1. up
2. down
3. up
4. down
5. 5°F
6. 2°F
7. 3°F
8. 5°F
9. Thurs., Fri, Sat.
10. Sun., Mon., Tues., Wed.

Page 113
1. up
2. down
3. up
4. up
5. 1 cap
6. 11 caps
7. 4 caps
8. 2 caps
9. Fri., Sat.
10. Sun., Tues., Thurs.

Page 114
square: 6, 7, 8, 9, 10, 11
triangle: 8, 9, 10, 11, 12, 13, 14, 15, 16
1. 9 stickers
2. 13 stickers
3. 2 stickers
4. 6 stickers
5. 105 stickers
6. 20 stickers
7. 5 stickers
8. 5 stickers
9. $\triangle - 5 = \square$

Page 115
square: 9, 10, 11, 12, 13, 14
triangle: 3, 4, 5, 6, 7, 8, 9, 10, 11
1. 4 football cards
2. 8 football cards
3. 5 football cards
4. 12 football cards
5. 17 football cards
6. 103 football cards
7. 3 football cards
8. 3 football cards
9. $\triangle + 3 = \square$

Page 116
1. 4
2. 6
3. 8
4. 10
5. 12
6. 2
7. 12
8. 14
9. 16
10. 18

Page 117
1. 6
2. 2
3. 12
4. 8
5. 4
6. 4
7. 18
8. 14
9. 10
10. 6

Page 118
1. 4
2. Answers will vary.
3. 5
4. Answers will vary.
5. 9
6. 1
7. 0
8. 12
9. 15
10. 13
11. 4 triangles, because 20 > 16

Page 119
6 + 6; 3 + 3 + 6; 4 + 4 + 4; 1.–3. Answers will vary.
8 + 8; 8 + 4 + 4; 8 + 4 + 2 + 2; 4.–6. Answers will vary.